TEACH YOURSELF TO READ HEBREW

REVISED EDITION

Ethelyn Simon
and
Joseph Anderson

EKS PUBLISHING CO.
Albany, California

Consultants
Victoria Koltun Kelman
Cantor Bruce Benson
Susan Rattray

Editorial Assistant
Alan K. Lipton

Book Design
Irene Imfeld

ISBN 0-939144-11-5

Printed January 2000

1029A Solano Avenue
Albany, CA 94706
Phone: (510) 558-9200
Fax: (510) 558-9255
E-mail: EKS@wenet.net

P.O. Box 9750
Berkeley, CA 94709

TABLE OF CONTENTS

HEBREW EDUCATIONAL MATERIALS AVAILABLE FROM EKS PUBLISHING COMPANY

INTRODUCTION

Teach Yourself to Read Hebrew is designed specifically for the needs of adult beginners. Hebrew letters and vowels are presented simply, enabling students to advance rapidly. Students begin with single sounds, and then progress to syllables, whole words, and sentences from well-known prayers. Exercises included with each chapter provide opportunities to practice reading and writing skills.

Teach Yourself to Read Hebrew is divided into ten lessons, and a set of cassette tapes is available as a companion to the book. The tapes guide students through all material presented in the book, providing access to correct pronunciation as students progress. When used together, *Teach Yourself to Read Hebrew* and the cassette tapes offer a complete audiovisual introduction to reading Hebrew.

Teach Yourself to Read Hebrew can be used three different ways:

1. It may be used by a teacher or tutor. This is probably the most effective way to learn from the text; students are certain to learn correct pronunciation, and a teacher can give students additional guidance and motivation.

2. It may be used with the companion tape set available from EKS Publishing Company. The tape set will help students pronounce letters, vowels, syllables and words, serving as a teacher that is available at all times.

3. It may be used by itself. Without the aid of a teacher or the cassettes, learning to read Hebrew can be difficult. However, *Teach Yourself to Read Hebrew* clearly explains how to pronounce each Hebrew sound using examples from English, making it a self-teaching book.

This book teaches the Sephardic, or Middle-Eastern, pronunciation of Hebrew. Sephardic pronunciation is officially accepted by the State of Israel and is used all over the United States.

Once students know how to pronounce Hebrew, they may wish to learn how to translate it. EKS Publishing Company has several textbooks and teaching aids designed to teach Biblical and Prayerbook Hebrew to adult beginners. Call or write EKS Publishing for a free catalog.

There are several major differences between English and Hebrew.

ENGLISH	HEBREW
1. English is read from left to right.	**1.** Hebrew is read from right to left.
2. In the English alphabet, there are 26 letters: some are vowels (a, e, i, o, u), and some are consonants (b, c, d, g, etc.).	**2.** In the Hebrew alphabet, there are 22 letters, all of which are consonants. Vowels are dots and dashes added below and beside the consonants.
3. English has both capital and small letters.	**3.** The Hebrew alphabet has no capital letters.
4. English letters are never written differently when they appear at the end of a word.	**4.** Five Hebrew letters have a different form when they appear at the end of a word.
5. It is impossible to learn to read English without knowing the meaning of words, because letters and letter combinations can be pronounced in so many different ways. Examples: the letter **c** in the words **c**at and **c**ircle, and the letters **ough** in the words thr**ough** and c**ough.**	**5.** Hebrew consonants and vowels are *always* pronounced the same. Therefore it is possible to learn to read Hebrew without knowing the meaning of words.

LESSON 1

This lesson is an introduction to Hebrew consonants and vowels. You will learn three Hebrew letters, and one Hebrew vowel sound. By the end of this lesson, you will be able to read an important word in Hebrew. In Lesson 2, we will begin to introduce the rest of the Hebrew letters in alphabetical order.

In Hebrew, there are 22 different consonants. Three of these consonants are shown above. They are:

B as in **B**oy	בּ
SH as in **SH**ape	שׁ
T as in **T**all	ת

Hebrew vowels are shown by adding dots and dashes below or beside Hebrew consonants. Two Hebrew vowels are shown below. They are both added below Hebrew consonants, and are both pronounced in the same way. The X represents any Hebrew consonant.

a as in y**a**cht X̲ Xָ

When a Hebrew vowel is written underneath a Hebrew consonant, pronounce the consonant first, and then the vowel.

Always read Hebrew from right to left.

שָׁ = Xָ + שׁ ←

sha = a + sh ←

See if you can read the following combinations of letters and vowels introduced in this lesson.

Always read Hebrew from right to left.

Writing is an additional way to help you learn to read Hebrew letters. The chart below shows how to write the three Hebrew letters introduced in this lesson. The letters below are written in block print, which looks very much like printed Hebrew letters.

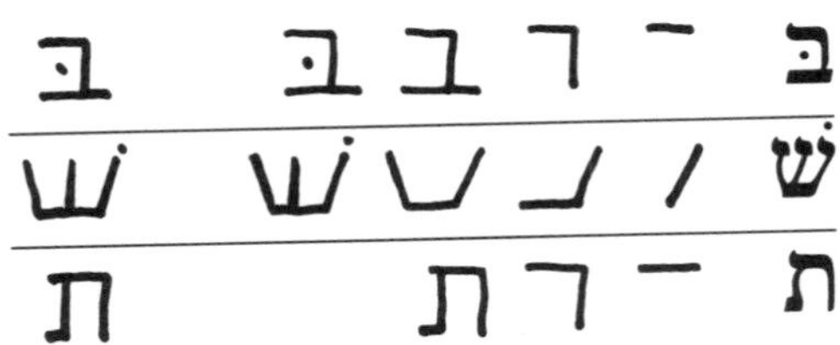

To help you fix the shapes of the Hebrew letters firmly in your mind, we will teach you how to write each letter as it is introduced. The diagram above shows you how to write the letters בּ, שׁ, and ת, step by step.

Exercises

1. Write one line of each new letter with each of the vowel sounds you have learned, sounding the letters with the vowels as you write them.
Examples:

2. Copy the following combinations of letters and vowels, saying each one aloud as you write it.

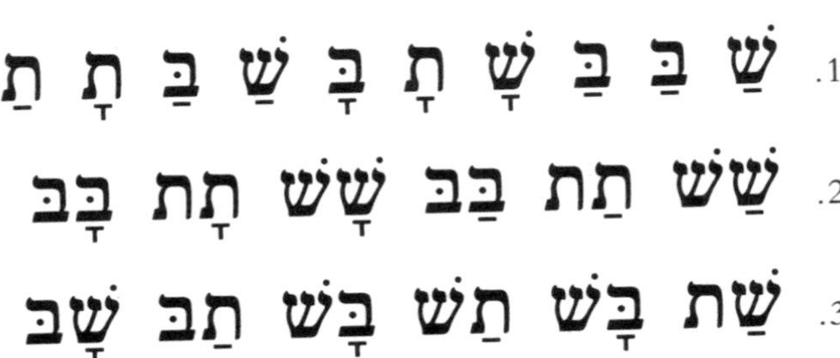

3. Write five English words that begin with the same sound as each of the Hebrew consonants you have learned so far.

Examples: toy ת bell בּ shoe שׁ

4. Write the Hebrew vowel and consonant combinations that sound like the following English words.

1. Bob 2. tot 3. shot

5. Read the following combinations of letters and vowels aloud.

1. שׁ שַׁ שָׁשַׁ שַׁבּ שַׁתַ שָׁבַּ

2. בּ בַּ בָּבַּ בַּשׁ בַּתַ בָּשַׁ בַּתָ

3. ת תַ תָתַ תַשׁ תַשַׁ תָבַּ תָשָׁ

4. שַׁבּ תַבּ בַּבּ שָׁת בָּת תַת

5. שָׁבַּ בָּשַׁ שָׁתַ תָשׁ בָּתַ תָבַּ

6. שָׁשַׁבּ בָּשַׁבּ תָשַׁבּ שָׁשַׁת שַׁבָּ

7. בָּבַּשׁ שָׁבַּשׁ תָבַּשׁ בָּבָּת בַּת

8. שַׁבָּת בַּת שַׁבָּת שַׁשׁ שַׁבָּת

The three-letter word repeated in line 8 may be familiar to you. It is the word **shabbat**, "Sabbath".

LESSON 2

In the first lesson you were introduced to three Hebrew consonants and one Hebrew vowel sound:

a Xַ a Xָ t ת sh שׁ b בּ

You also learned to read combinations of vowels and consonants. In this lesson we will begin to teach you the letters of the Hebrew alphabet in alphabetical order. The letters shown below are the first letters of the Hebrew alphabet. You have already learned the letter בּ in the first lesson. This letter is pronounced differently when it does not have a dot in it.

Silent letter	א
B as in **B**oy	בּ
V as in **V**ine	ב
G as in **G**irl	ג
D as in **D**oor	ד

In many examples in this book, Hebrew letter and vowel combinations are shown with English words that have the same sound. This will make it easier for you to check your pronunciation of new Hebrew letters and vowels as you learn them. For example, the words below show you how to pronounce the letter **א**.

The letter **א** is a silent letter. When it appears with a vowel under it, simply pronounce the vowel. When it appears without a vowel, do not pronounce it at all.

shah = **שָׁא**   odd = **אָד** ←

Vowels The vowel sound for this lesson is:

ee as in b**ee** Xִי Xִ

This vowel may be written in two ways:

1. As a dot under a consonant.

בִּ = Xִ + **בּ** ←

bee = ee + b

2. As a dot under a consonant, followed by a **י** after the consonant.

בִּי = Xִי + **בּ** ←

bee = ee + b

Read the following lines.

1. אִ אִי בִּ בִּי בִ בִי גִ גִי דִ דִי

2. דִי דַ בִ בִּ גָ גִי אִ אַ גִי דִ בָ

Dots in Hebrew Letters Dots often appear in Hebrew letters. Most letters are pronounced the same whether or not they have a dot in them.

tot = תַת = תַּת

deed = דִיד = דִּיד

got = גָת = גָּת

Three Hebrew letters are pronounced differently when they have a dot in them. You have already learned one of these letters: **בּ B** as in **B**oy or **ב V** as in **V**ine.

Below is a chart showing how to write the Hebrew letters in this lesson.

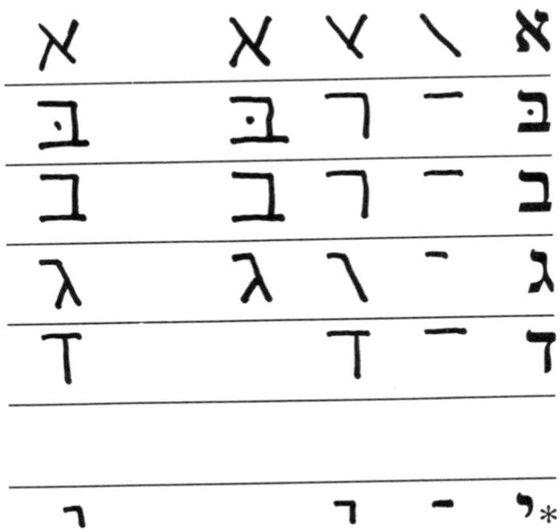

Letter	Written
א	א
בּ	בּ
ב	ב
ג	ג
ד	ד
י*	י

*You learned this letter י in this lesson as part of the vowel אִי **ee.** It also has other uses, which you will learn later.

Exercises

1. Write one line of each new letter with each of the vowel sounds you have learned, sounding the letters with the vowels as you write them.

2. Pronounce the letters in each line below. Circle the letters in each line that are the same as the letter in the box.

1. [א] א בּ ב ג ד שׁ ת
2. [בּ] בּ ד ג ב שׁ בּ ת
3. [ב] בּ שׁ ד א ב ת ג
4. [ג] ת ג א שׁ ג ד בּ
5. [ד] ב ד בּ ג ד ת שׁ
6. [שׁ] ג ב ת שׁ בּ א ד
7. [ת] א ג שׁ ת ב ד ב
8. [א] ב א ת ד שׁ א ג
9. [ג] שׁ ב ת ג בּ ד ג

3. In each pair of lines below, match the printed letters with the block letters.

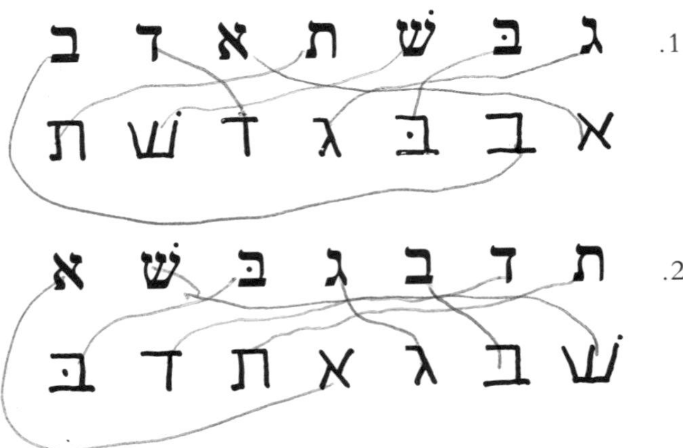

4. Copy the following combinations of letters and vowels, saying each one aloud as you write.

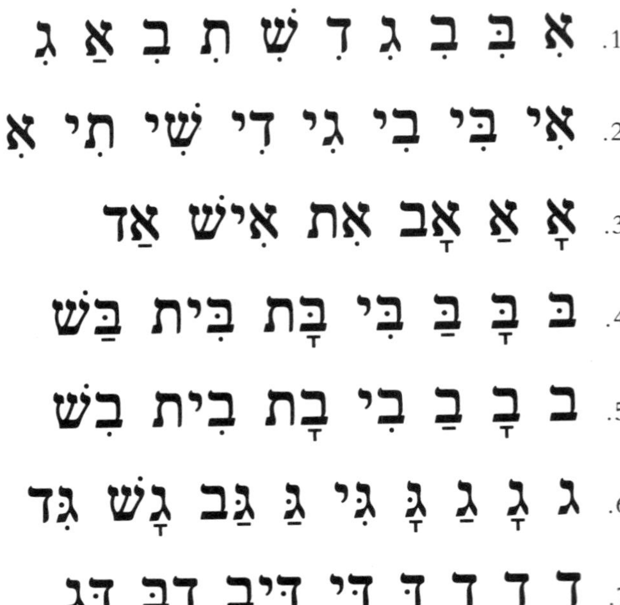

5. In the line below, taken from the beginning of the Kaddish prayer, circle all the letters you have learned so far.

יתגדל ויתקדש שמה רבא

6. Write the Hebrew vowel and consonant combinations that sound like the following English words.

1.	beet	5.	T.V.	9.	got	13.	shah
2.	dot	6.	sheet	10.	shot	14.	deed
3.	tea	7.	tot	11.	Eve	15.	bead
4.	she	8.	eat	12.	odd	16.	Bob

7. The following words are all real Hebrew words. Read them aloud.

1. אָב אַבָּא אָבִי אָבַד אִבַּד
2. אָדַשׁ בָּאִישׁ אִישִׁי אִישׁ
3. בִּי בָּאַשׁ בָּגַד בַּג בַּד
4. בָּא בָּאתָ בָּאתִי בָּאת בַּת
5. גַּב גַּבִּי גָּג גָּדַד גָּדִי גַּת
6. דָּאג דָּאַב דָּאַג דִּבַּת דָּג
7. תָּבִיא תָּשָׁב שָׁב תָּשִׁיב
8. שָׁבִית שָׁבַת בַּשַּׁבָּת שַׁבָּת

Words from Our Tradition

In each lesson we will give you translations of several words that you have read in the final exercise. You do not need to learn these words, although you may recognize some of them. They are included for your enjoyment and interest.

comes	=	בָּא	Sabbath	=	שַׁבָּת
man	=	אִישׁ	father	=	אָב
daughter	=	בַּת	my father	=	אָבִי

Learning Hints and Suggestions

We suggest that you use flashcards while learning Hebrew letters and vowels. These are available from EKS Publishing, or you may make your own. Write the letters and vowels that you have learned on index cards. As you learn new letters and vowels, make flashcards for them too. Flashcards can be used in a number of ways. Here are a few suggestions:

1. See how many combinations of letters and vowels you can create. Read each one.

2. Work with another person, making combinations and asking one another to read them.

3. See how many English words you can create with the letters and vowels you have. (See exercise 6 on page 13.)

Hebrew letters sometimes have dots in the middle, but there are only a few cases in which the dot will change the way a letter is pronounced. You have already learned one of these. We will point out the rest in later chapters.

LESSON 3

ה ו ז ח ט

These are the letters and vowels you have already learned:

d ד g ג v ב b בּ א

t ת sh שׁ

ee Xִי ee Xִ a Xַ a Xָ

In this lesson you will learn five new Hebrew letters.

H as in **H**ouse	ה
V as in **V**ine	ו
Z as in **Z**ebra	ז
CH as in Ba**CH**	ח
T as in **T**all	ט

The letter ח is pronounced with a rasping **H** sound, as in the word **CH**allah, or the German pronunciation of the word Ba**CH**.

Look-Alike Letters

Some Hebrew letters look very much alike. You must study these letters carefully, so that you will be able to tell them apart. There are three pairs of look-alike letters introduced in this lesson.

Notice the difference between the letter ה **H** as in **H**ouse and the letter ח **CH** as in Ba**CH**. The letter ה has a gap on the left side. The letter ח does not have a gap.

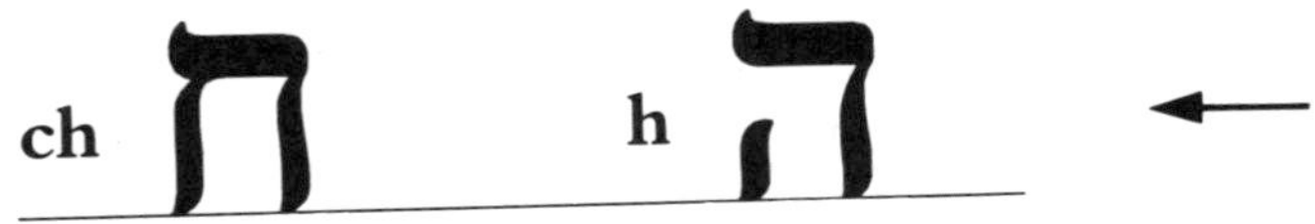

Notice the difference between the letter ת **T** and the letter ח **CH** as in Ba**CH**. The letter ת has a toe at the bottom of the left leg. The letter ח does not have a toe.

Notice the difference between the letter ו **V** and the letter ז **Z**. The letter ו is smooth at the top of the right side. The letter ז has a projection at the top of the right side.

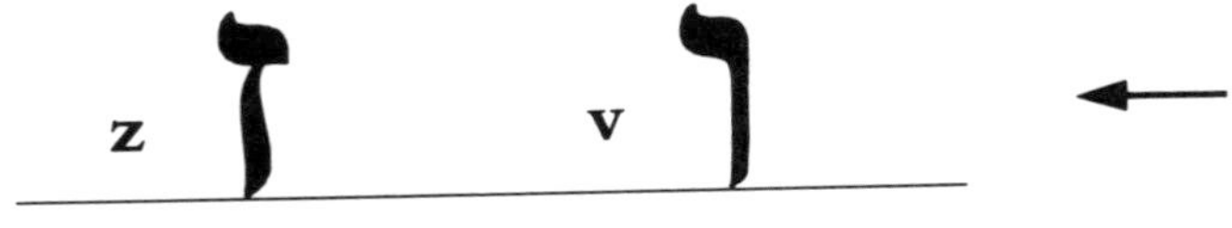

Read the following line aloud.

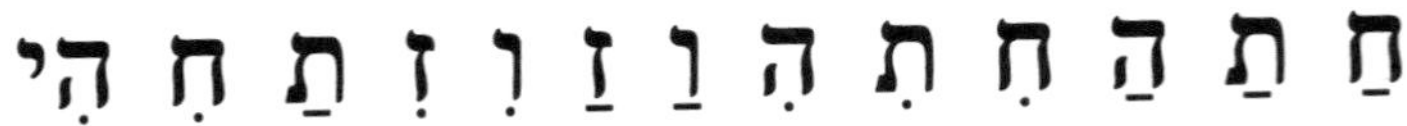

Sound-Alike Letters Some Hebrew letters have the same sound. The letters ב and ו are both pronounced **V** as in **V**ine.

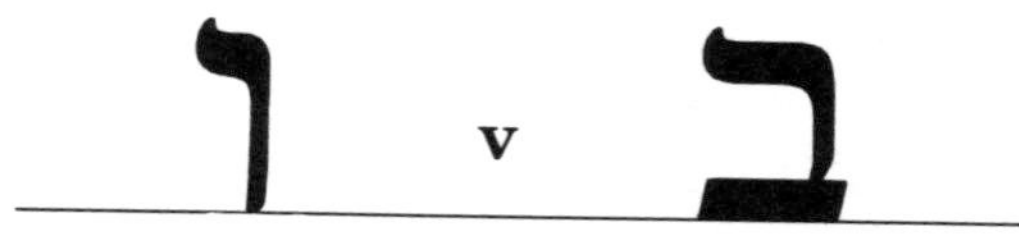

The letters ת and ט are both pronounced **T** as in **T**all.

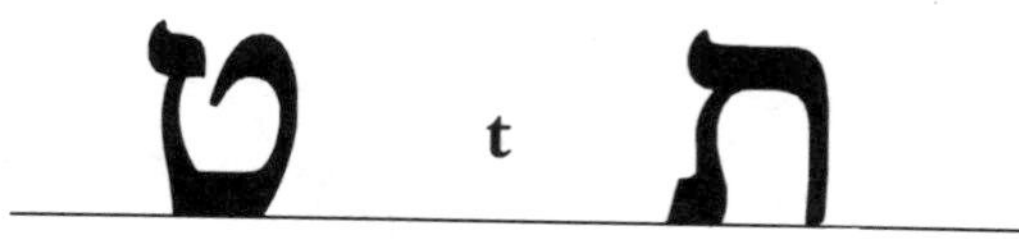

Read the following lines aloud.

1. בָ וָ בַ וַ בִּי וִ בִיו בִּיו בִּיב וַו
2. טָט תָּת תִּיט טִית תַּט תַח טָה
3. חָ תָ חַ תַ חַ הָ תַ חָ תַת חַח הָה
4. הִ חִ תִ חִ הִ תִ תִ חִ חִת תִה חִח
5. וַ זַ וִ זִ וָ זִי וִ וַז זִיו וִיז בָז בַּו

The Letter ה When the letter ה appears at the end of a word, it is not pronounced.

shah = שָׂה

Vowels These are the vowels you have already learned:

Xָ Xַ Xִ Xִי

The vowel for this lesson is:

ay as in h**ay** Xֵ Xֵי

Like the vowel **ee**, the vowel **ay** may be written in two ways. It may be written as two dots under a consonant.

ה + Xֵ = הֵ ←

h + ay = hay

The vowel **ay** may also be written as two dots under a consonant, followed by a י.

ה + Xֵי = הֵי ←

h + ay = hay

Read the following lines aloud.

1. חֵ הֵ חֵי חִי הֵי הִי וֵ בֵ וִי בִי

2. טֵ טַ תֵי טָ תִ חִ הֵ תֵי טֵי חֵי

3. זֵ וֵ זֵי וֵי וִי זִ זַ וֵ וָ זֵי זֵיז זֵיו

4. הֵז וִז תֵו וֵית הִיו טֵיז טִי טַט

The chart below shows how to write the letters introduced in this lesson.

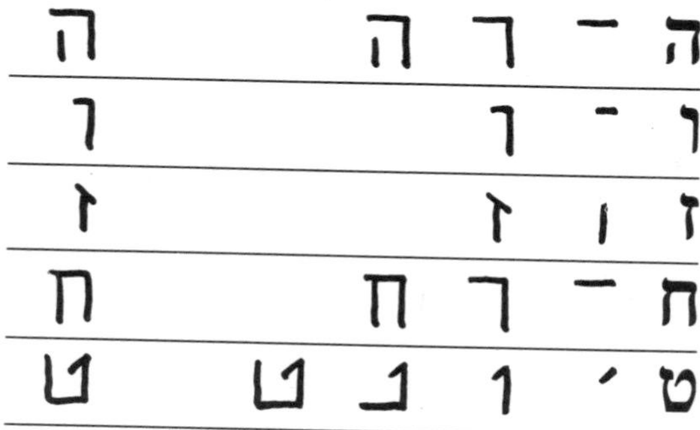

Exercises

1. Write one line of each new letter with each of the vowel sounds you have learned, sounding the letters with the vowels as you write them.

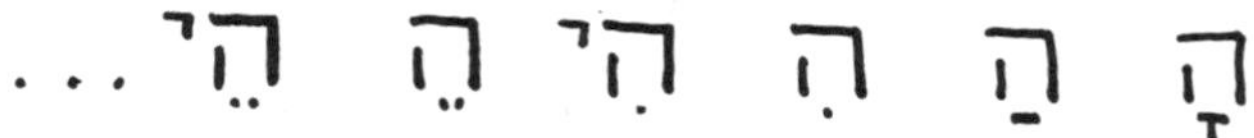

2. Match each Hebrew combination below with the English word that has the same sound.

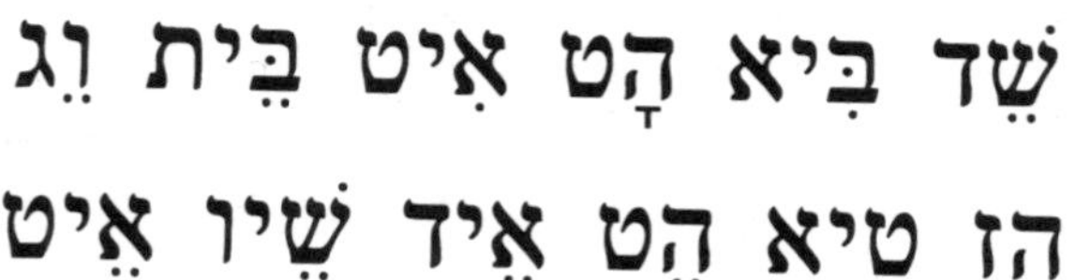

1. hot
2. eat
3. haze
4. shave
5. aid
6. tea
7. ate
8. bee
9. bait
10. hate
11. shade
12. vague

3. Pronounce the letters in each line. Circle the letters that have the same sound as the English letters in the boxes.

4. Read the following combinations of letters and vowels aloud.

1. אֵי בֵּ בֵי גֵ דֵי הֵי וֵ זֵי חִי טִי
2. ה הָ הִי הֵ הֵי הָד הֵישׁ הֵיד הִח
3. ו וָ וִי וֵ וֵי וָשׁ וֵיג וַת וִיד וִו
4. ז זָ זִי זֵ זֵי זָת זֵישׁ זֵיג זִיו זִח
5. ח חָ חֵ חִי חָג חַז חֵה חִית
6. ט טָ טִ טֵ טֵי טָט טִשׁ טִיד טָת

5. Read the following Hebrew letter combinations and circle the ones that sound like English words.

1. בִּיט בַּת בֵּיט בְּהֵב בֵּיהָ
2. טֵיב גֵּיו גֵּיז דֵּיב שֵׁיב שֵׁיו
3. אַוִד גַּוִד בַּוִד טַוִד בִּיד דָּוִד
4. גֵּית בֵּח הֵיט דֵּית בֵּח חֵת
5. שֵׁחַה שָׁחַת שִׁיט שָׁת שַׁבָּת שֵׁדִי

6. Read the following Hebrew letter combinations and circle the ones that sound alike in each line.

1. אַבִיב בָּבִיב גָּבִיב אָבִיו אָב
2. אַתָּה אֵזָה אֵגָה אָטָ אֵוָה אָח
3. הִיא הַבַּת הַזַט הַבֵּת הָחֵט הַבֵּט
4. חִיט חִיז הִיו חִטָה הִבָה חִית
5. גָּדִישׁ הַדִישׁ תַּדִישׁ חַדִישׁ הַדִשׁ
6. בֵּית דֵּיט הֵית טֵית הֵיט חֵית

7. In the following phrases, taken from well-known prayers, circle all the letters you have learned.

וטוב ויפה הדבר הזה . . .

הנה מה טוב שבת אחים גם יחד.

8. The following words are all real Hebrew words. Read them aloud until you can read them easily.

1. אָבִיו אָהֵב אָז אָח אֵיד אֵשׁ
2. בַּז בִּזָּה בָּטַח גֵּו גַּב בֵּית
3. גַּו גָּדִישׁ גֵּהָה גֵּז גִּזָּה גָּזֵז
4. דִּבָּה דָּגָה אַתָּה דָּשׁ דָּתֵי דָּוִד
5. הִיא הָאָב חָדִיד הַב הַבֵּט הָגָה
6. זָבַח זִבַּח זָהָב זִו זָבַת זָבַד
7. זֵד חִבֵּשׁ חָגָב חַד טָא חָג
8. חִטָּה חִטֵּא חַטָּאת חָשַׁב חָדָשׁ

Words from Our Tradition

festival, holiday = חַג   David = דָּוִד

house (of) = בֵּית   new = חָדָשׁ

you = אַתָּה

Learning Hints and Suggestions

1. The letter ה in Hebrew is treated very much like the letter **H** in English. When **H** comes at the end of a word such as **hurrah** or **Sarah**, it is always silent. Even if you wanted to pronounce the **H** at the end of a word, you would find it almost impossible. In the same way, a ה at the end of a Hebrew word is always silent.

2. Look-alike letters are found in English as well as Hebrew. Remember how many children have trouble seeing the difference between **b** and **d**.

3. English, like Hebrew, has many sound-alike letters. Think of **can** and **kitty**, or of **George** and **Joe**.

4. Here is a good way to remember the difference between the letters ה and ח. The letter with an opening, ה, has lots of room for breath to escape, making a soft, breathing sound **H**. The letter with no opening, ח, has no room for breath to escape, so it comes out with a rasping **CH** sound.

LESSON 4

י כּ כ ל מ

These are the letters and vowels you have already learned:

א	בּ b	ב v	ג g	ד d	ה h
ו v	ז z	ח ch	ט t	שׁ sh	ת t
Xָ a	Xַ a	Xִ ee	Xִי ee	Xֵ ay	Xֵי ay

In this lesson, you will learn four new letters. One letter, the letter כ, has two different sounds. When it has a dot inside it, it is pronounced **K** as in **K**itty. When it does not have a dot inside it, it is pronounced with a rasping **H** sound, as in **CH**allah or Ba**CH**.

Y as in **Y**es	י
K as in **K**itty	כּ
CH as in Ba**CH**	כ
L as in **L**ook	ל
M as in **M**other	מ

The Letter י Like the English letter **Y**, י can be used as part of a vowel, or as a consonant.

yacht	=	יָט	body	=	בָּדִי
yea	=	יֵא	lady	=	לֵדִי

Look-Alikes Notice the difference between the letter בּ **B** and the letter כּ **K**. The letter בּ has a small projection on the lower right-hand side. The letter כּ is rounded.

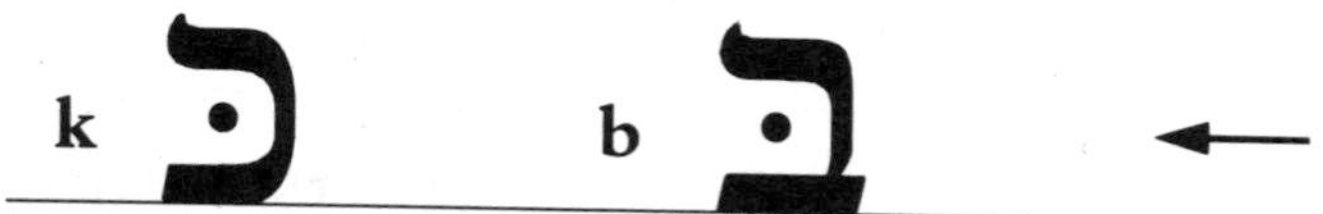

Notice the difference between the letter ו **V** and the letter י **Y**. The letter ו is longer than the letter י.

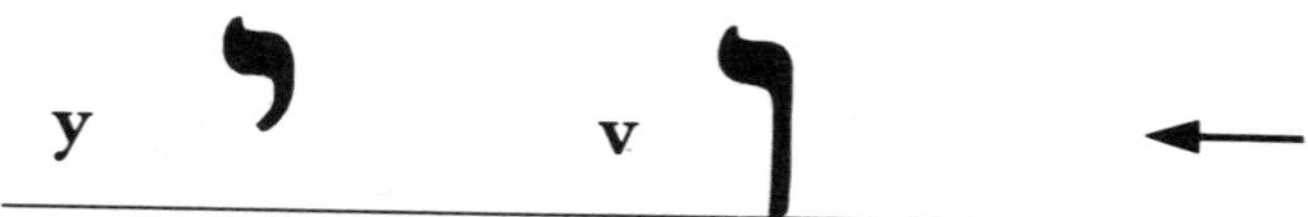

Notice the difference between the letter מ **M** and the letter ט **T**. The letter מ has a small gap at the bottom. The letter ט has a small gap at the top.

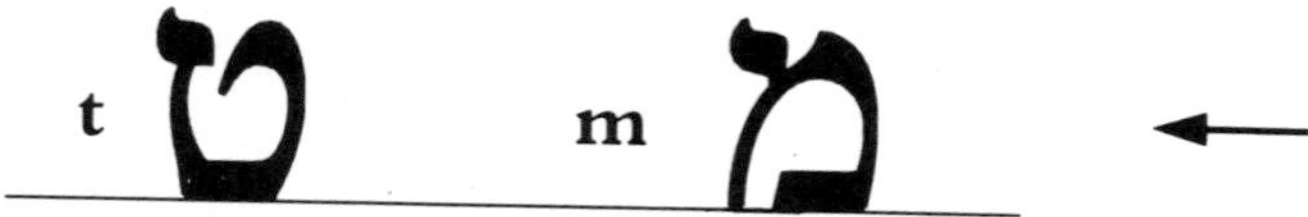

Sound-Alikes The letter ח and the letter כ (when it does not have a dot) have the same sound, **CH** as in Ba**CH**.

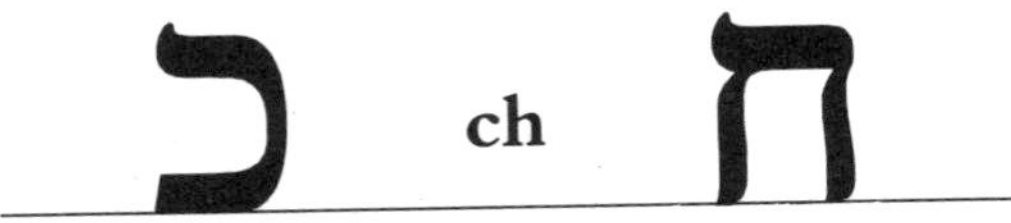

Read the following lines.

1. כַּ כַ הָ כָ כַּ חַ כַ חָ הַ חִי כִי
2. וַ יַ יָ יִ וִ יֵ וֵי וָשׁ יָשׁ וֵישׁ
3. מִ טִ טִ מָ מַ טֵ טִ מִי טֵי מִט
4. הִ חָ תֵ חֵי תִי הִי תָּ חִ הֵ
5. וִ זִי בִּי בֵ חֵי הֵי תֵי טֵי
6. בַּ כַּ כָ בָ בֵּ כֵ כִּ בִּי כִי בִי
7. יִ וִ יַ זַ וַ יֵ וֵ דֵ גֵ יָ וָ זִ וִ
8. כִּשׁ חָשׁ בִּחָה בִּכָה כַּב בַּו
9. מִי מֵי טִי מָא אָט מִט תֵּט

Below is a chart showing how to write the Hebrew letters in this lesson.

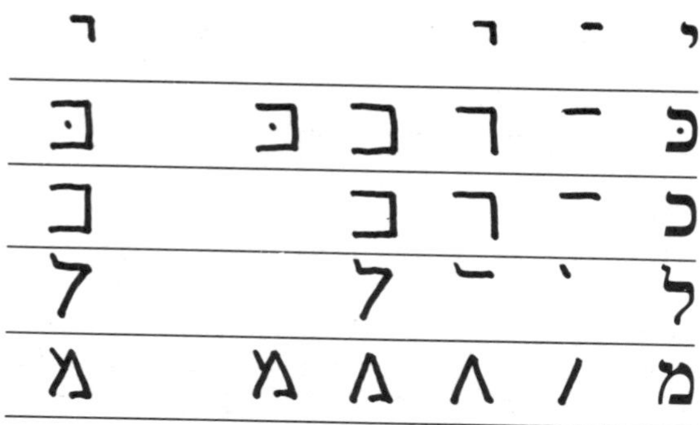

Exercises

1. Write one line of each new letter with each of the vowel sounds you have learned, sounding the letters with the vowels as you write them.

2. In the pairs of lines below, match the printed letters with the block print letters.

3. Circle the letters in each line that have the same sound as the English letters in the boxes. Pronounce all the letters in each line.

Y	ו	ז	י	ו	ד	י	ו	ז
K	ה	ב	כּ	ח	כּ	ה	כ	בּ
CH	ד	ח	ת	כ	ד	ל	כּ	כ
M	ט	מ	כ	בּ	מ	ט	ב	מ
T	ח	ת	ט	ה	ת	כ	מ	ט
L	ט	מ	ל	שׁ	כ	ח	ל	א
H	מ	ג	א	ה	ט	ח	ה	ת

4. Read all the following Hebrew letter combinations and circle the ones that sound like English words.

1. טַדִי בָּדִי יַדִי כָּדִי כַדִי חַדִי
2. כֵּיל טֵיל חֵיל הֵיל דֵּיל כֵיל
3. לֵזִי דֵּזִי מֵבִּי לֵכִי מֵחִי כֵּתִּי
4. מַמִּי לַמִּי יָמִי יָכָה יֵכָּה יִכָה

5. Spell the following English words with Hebrew letters.

1.	mate	4.	gate	7.	shade	10.	leave
2.	maze	5.	cave	8.	hot	11.	late
3.	tail	6.	me	9.	heat	12.	cot

6. Read aloud all the following letter combinations. In each line copy the combinations that have the same sound.

1. זָה וַה בָא בָּח גָּח וָא אָו אָב
2. בִּיז כִּיז בִּיו בִּיג כִּו בִּי בִּב
3. לָהַב לָאָב לַחַח לָאָח לָכַח לַח
4. אַיִל אַוַל אַוִל אַיַל אַזַל אָבַל
5. תָּמִשׁ חַמִשׁ הָמִשׁ טָמִשׁ מָטִישׁ
6. זָת וַת וַה זָה וָח זַט כַּת זַו וַו
7. בִּיד בִּיָד בַּיִב כִּיו בִּיב בַּיִו וִיוֵי
8. לִישׁ לֵישׁ דֵּישׁ דָּיִשׁ לִשׁ לָשׁ
9. מֵיטִי מֵלִי מֵיזָה מֵתִי מֵישִׁי מִבִי
10. וֵייִן בֵּייִן וַייִב וֵייִב וַיִי וַיִב וַב

7. In the following phrase from a prayer called **Mi Chamocha**, circle all the letters you have learned so far.

משה ובני ישראל לך ענו שירה
בשמחה רבה, ואמרו כלם:
מי כמכה באלים. . .

8. The following words are all real Hebrew words. Read them aloud until you can read them easily.

1. גָּאַל גָּדֵל גָּמָּל גָּבַל גָּלִיל גָּדַל
2. דָּאִית הָמִיט דָּבָאת דָּגִית דָּמִי
3. יִשֵׁב מִלֵּא כִּחֵשׁ שִׁלַּח אִמֵּת הִלֵּל
4. הָיָה חָיָה חַיִל חִמָּה הִמָּה
5. טַח טִיט מִטִיט טַל טָמֵא טַלִית
6. יָבֵשׁ יָבָל יָד מִיָּד יָחִיל יָלַד
7. כִּי כָּזָב כָּבֵד כָּחַשׁ כֵּהָה כָּלֵב
8. לָהּ לֵאָה לִי לִבִּי לָכִישׁ לִמַּד

Words from Our Tradition

hand	=	יָד	camel	=	גָּמָל
Leah	=	לֵאָה	tallit	=	טַלִית
bride	=	כַּלָה	bread	=	חַלָה

Learning Hints and Suggestions

1. An easy way to think of the letter מ is that the **m**ilk is running out of the bottom. And nothing runs out of the letter ט, which is a **t**eapot with its opening on the top.

2. You are now more than halfway through the alphabet. There may be some letters that you are having a little difficulty remembering. Take the flashcards of those letters, write the English pronunciation of each letter on its card, and place them where you can't help looking at them several times a day (your bathroom mirror, over your kitchen sink, etc.). You will be surprised how soon you will find them imprinted in your mind.

3. Open your prayerbook to any page. Count the number of times each familiar Hebrew letter appears in the first ten lines. For example, you might find the letter א 20 times, the letter ב 12 times, and so on.

4. Using the same page of the prayerbook, look for Hebrew words that you can read. On most pages you will find at least five or six.

LESSON 5

נ ס ע

For the first time in this lesson, the review of letters and vowels you have already learned is given without the English sounds. If you are having any difficulty with any of these letters or vowels, or would simply like to review them to give yourself more confidence, go back to previous chapters and be sure you are thoroughly familiar with them before going on.

In this lesson you will learn three new letters.

N as in **N**ow	נ
S as in **S**un	ס
Silent letter	ע

Sound-Alikes The letter ע, like the letter א, is a silent letter. When א or ע appear with a vowel under them, simply pronounce the vowel. When they appear without a vowel, do not pronounce them at all.

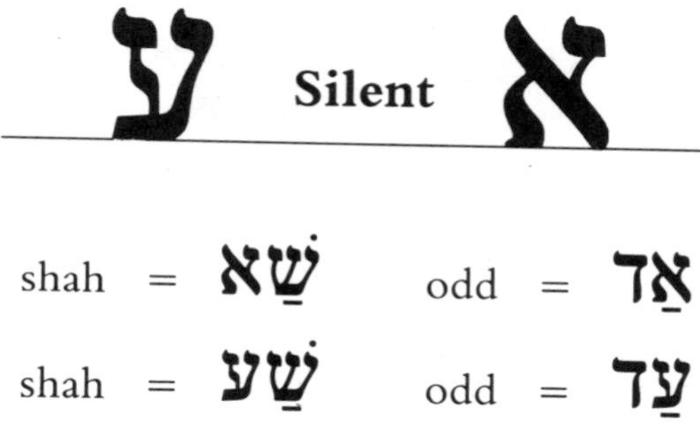

Look-Alikes Notice the difference between the letter ג **G** and the letter נ **N**. The letter ג has a "cloven hoof", and the letter נ has a flat foot.

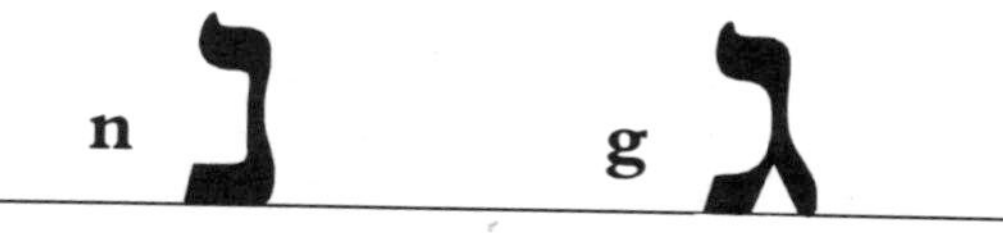

Read the following lines aloud.

Vowels These are the vowel sounds you have already learned:

אָ אַ אִ אִי אֵ אֵי

The vowel sound for this lesson is:

eh as in b**e**d אֶ

The vowel **eh** as in b**e**d is normally written as three dots underneath a Hebrew consonant.

בֶּד = אֶד + בּ

bed = ed + b

get = גֶּת   head = הֶד

Read the following lines aloud.

.1 אֶ בֶּ סֶ דֶ מֶ טֶ לֶ עֶ גֶ נֶ

.2 בֶּע גַּא נֶה עֶח הִיא הֶע חַה

The chart below shows how to write the letters introduced in this lesson.

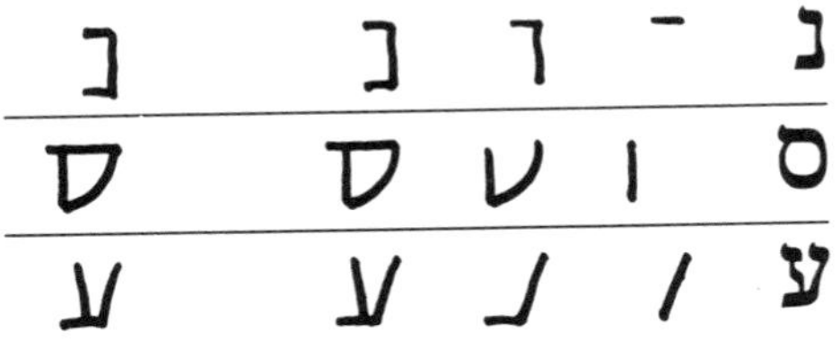

נ	נ
ס	ס
ע	ע

Exercises

1. Write one line of each new letter with each of the vowel sounds you have learned, sounding the letters with the vowels as you write them.

2. In the pair of lines below, match the printed letters with the block letters.

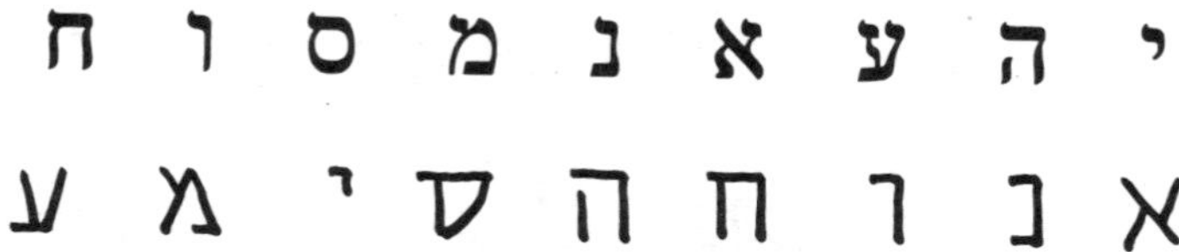

3. In each line, circle the letters that have the same sound as the English letters in the boxes. Pronounce each letter in each line.

4. Write the following English words with Hebrew letters. If possible, spell more than one way.

1. seed
2. deal
3. date
4. yes
5. let
6. net
7. niece
8. leave
9. yet
10. lease
11. mesh
12. neat

5. Read the combinations below and copy each combination of letters that sound alike.

1. סָבָא סַבֵּב סָבִיב בַּסַּד סַוִיו
2. אֵית עֶט עִיט אֶת אֵיט אֵת עַט
3. נְטֶה נָטָה נָמָע נִיתֶע נִיסֶא
4. עֶבֶד עִבו אֶוֶד דָּוִד עֶנֶד עֶגֶד

6. Read and enjoy the following combinations.

סִי בֶּתִי עִת.

עִת, בֶּתִי, עִת.

סִי בֶּתִי עִת כִּישׁ.

עִת כִּישׁ, בֶּתִי, עִת כִּישׁ.

סִי בָּבּ עִת בֶּתִיז כִּישׁ.

סִי בֶּתִי בִּית בָּבּ.

7. The following words are all real Hebrew words. Read them aloud.

1. עֶבֶד עֵגֶל עֵדָה עֵינֵי עָנָה עִכֵּס
2. סֵבֶל סִחָה סָחַב סִיג סֶלָה סָלַח
3. נִכָּה נֶכֶד נִסָּה נִסִּי נֶגֶב נָחַל
4. מָלֵא מֶלַח מַכָּה מִיכַל מִטָּה מָוֶת
5. לָאַט לִבִּי לָעַד לָמָּה לַמֵּד לֵוִי
6. כָּבֵד כָּלִיל כֶּלֶב כָּתַב כִּסֵּא כָּלָה
7. יֵשׁ יָשַׁב יֶלֶד יָדַע יָחִיד יָעָה
8. טָמֵא טָבַע טֶבַח טֵבֵת טָלֶה טֶנֶא
9. חַיִל חֵלֶב חָטַב חַיָּה חִיאֵל חַיַּת
10. זַכָּה זֶה זָבַח זֶבֶד זָהָב
11. וִיחִי וָו וַיֵּאת וָהֵב וָלָד הִיא
12. דָּשָׁא דַּעַת דֶּלֶת הֵטִיל הִזִּיל

Words from Our Tradition

Levy	=	לֵוִי	Negev	=	נֶגֶב
forgive	=	סָלַח	year	=	שָׁנָה

Learning Hints and Suggestions

By this time you have learned about three-quarters of the letters in the Hebrew alphabet. It is very important that you review the letters and vowels you have learned. You should spend some time in review every day. We introduce the letters at a slower rate in Lessons 5 through 7. Because of this, you will be able to learn the last few letters easily. At the same time, you will have a better opportunity to review the letters and vowels that you have already learned.

Here are some reminders of ways to review letters:

1. We suggest that you continue using flashcards. Some suggestions for use are given on page 14. Flashcards make it quick and easy for you to review the letters you have learned.

2. Write the letters you know. Writing and pronouncing the letters you have already learned is the best way to ensure that you remember them. Write the letters in order; make up combinations of letters and vowels; write English words using Hebrew spelling—the main thing is that you write!

3. Use your prayerbook to practice reading and recognizing sounds and letters. By now you can recognize and pronounce more than half of the vowel sounds and letters on each page. This exercise will also give you a beginning ability to recognize letters you have not yet learned, so that when we introduce them, they will be easier for you to remember.

4. The vowel אֶ **eh** as in b**e**d is sometimes written אֶי. It is still pronounced **eh** as in b**e**d.

LESSON 6

These are the letters and vowels you have already learned:

In this lesson you will learn three new letters.

P as in **P**eople	פּ
F as in **F**ood	פ
TS as in Nu**TS**	צ
K as in **K**itty	ק

The letter פ is pronounced in two different ways. When it has a dot in it, פּ, it is pronounced **P** as in **P**eople. When it does not have a dot in it, פ, it is pronounced **F** as in **F**ood.

You have now learned all three Hebrew letters that have different pronunciations with and without a dot in the center.

B as in **B**oy	בּ
V as in **V**ine	ב
K as in **K**itty	כּ
CH as in Ba**CH**	כ
P as in **P**eople	פּ
F as in **F**ood	פ

Read the following lines aloud.

1. כֶּ בֶּ פֶּ כִי בִ פִּ פַּ כַ פַ פֵּי פִּ
2. בָּא אָב אָכָה כָּה אָפָה פָּה
3. בֵּי כֵּי פֵּי לֵבַה לֵכַה לֵפַה
4. צֶ צֶל צַשׁ צִד צֵית מַצָּה בֵּצָה
5. קַפַה קַבַה קַכַה פִּק בִּק כִּק
6. כֵּצָה צַכָה צָבָא פִּצָה צָפִיד אֵצֵב
7. קַד דִּק קֵצָה כָּכָה בָּבָה פָּפָה צִיק

Look-Alikes The letter צ **TS** as in nu**TS** looks like two letters you have already learned. Notice the difference between the silent letter א and the letter צ **TS** as in nu**TS**. The letter א has two legs and two arms. The letter צ has one leg with a flat foot and two arms.

Notice the difference between the silent letter ע and the letter צ **TS** as in nu**TS**. The arms of the letter ע branch at the bottom. The arms of the letter צ branch in the middle.

Sound-Alikes The letter ק has the same sound as the letter כּ with a dot.

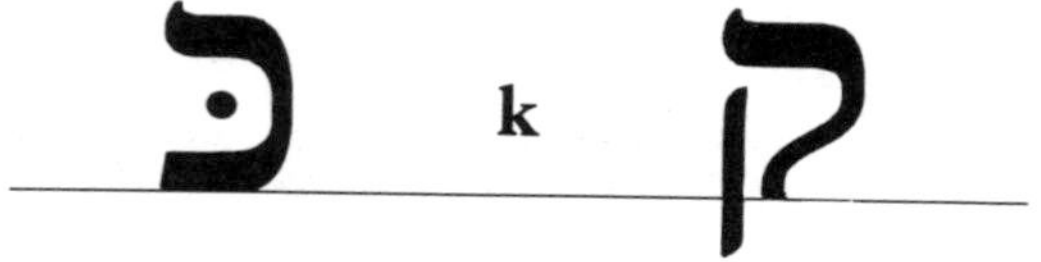

Read the following lines aloud.

Vowels These are the vowels you have already learned:

Xָ Xַ Xִ Xִי Xֵ Xֵי Xֶ

The vowel sound for this lesson is:

o as in l**o**w Xוֹ Xֹ

The vowel sound **o** is written as the letter ו with a dot on top וֹ, appearing to the left of another Hebrew consonant.

לוֹ = Xוֹ + ל

low = o + l

boat = בּוֹט show = שׁוֹא

The vowel sound **o** is also written as a dot to the upper left of a Hebrew consonant.

לֹ = Xֹ + ל

low = o + l

boat = בֹּט show = שֹׁא

Read the following lines aloud.

1. אוֹ שׁוֹ מוֹ קוֹ בּוֹ דוֹ לוֹא גּוֹת
2. דֹ הֹ זֹ חֹ שֹׁב נֹק סֹד צֹג פֹּה
3. פּוֹק פֹּק צוֹק צֹק כּוֹקַה כֹּלַה

Look-Alikes The vowel וֹ **o** looks almost exactly like the letter ו **V**, which you have already learned. The vowel וֹ **o** will always have a dot on top וֹ.

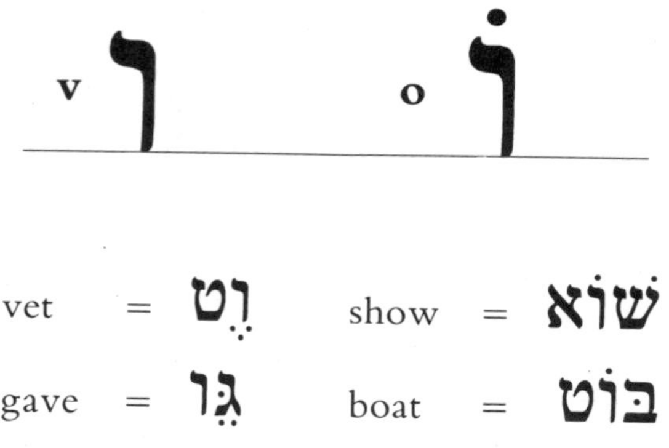

Read the following lines.

1. בּוֹג וֵג בּוֹד וַד בּוֹל וְל בּוֹט וֵט
2. מוֹה מֹה מַוֶה מוֹד מַוֵד מוֹא מֹוַע
3. לוֹ וַלוֹ בּוֹ וַבּוֹ סוֹ וַסוֹ זוֹ וַזוֹ

Below is a chart showing how to write the Hebrew letters in this lesson.

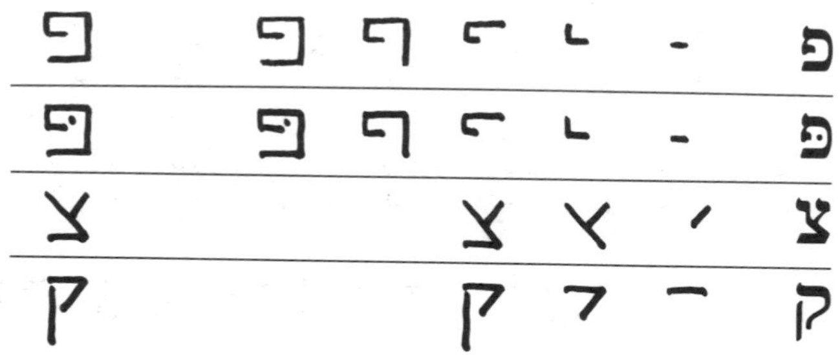

Exercises

1. Write one line of each new letter with each of the vowel sounds you have learned, sounding the letters with the vowels as you write them.

2. In the pair of lines below, match the printed letters with the block print letters.

פ ק ד ה צ ו א ח

ד צ ק פ ה ח ו א

3. Pronounce each letter in each line. Copy the letters in each line that sound like the English letter in the box.

4. Spell each of the following words in as many ways as you can, using Hebrew letters.

1. low	3. goal	5. show	7. matza	9. Coca-Cola
2. pot	4. pole	6. poke	8. pizza	10. keys

5. Read the following letter combinations and circle the words that sound alike.

1. פַּט פִּיט פּוֹנִי פּוֹת פֵּיט פִּת
2. חִפָּה הִפּוֹא תִּיפָּה הִיפֹּה חִפּוֹ
3. צַדֵה אֵצֹת מַצוֹת עֵצוֹט צַדִּיק
4. כִּיפָּה כֵּפַּא קִפַּע קֵפֹּה כִּיפּוֹ
5. אֹמֵד אוֹכֶל עֹחַל עֹבֵד עוֹחֶל
6. קַבֵּל קַבֵּס קָלַח כַּשֵׂק קַטֵב כַּתֵיו
7. אֵקֹל תֵּכַּל יֵקֹל נֵקַל טֵכַּל מֵכֹּל
8. אֶדַּל תִּדַּל יִדֹּל טִידַל נִדַּל נֹדֵל
9. קִיו כּוֹ כִּיוֹ קָוֶה קִוָא כִּיוַ כֵּיוָה
10. פּוֹ פֹּא פֹּה פֹּח פֹּת פּוֹט פִּה פִּוֹא

6. Read and enjoy the following dialogue.

מַה סֶד: ״הִיז אֵי מִינְי.״

פַּה סֶד: ״נוֹ! הִיז נַת אֵי

מִינְי. הִיא מֵיד אֵי נִית בּוֹת.

הִיא מֵיד אֵי יָט. הִיא גֵּב מִי

אֵי טִיבְי. הִיא גֵּב מִי דוֹ. אוֹ

נוֹ! הִיז נַת אֵי מִינְי.״

7. Read the following prayerbook words and phrases.

1. אֶת אוֹת אוֹתוֹת אוֹהֵב אֶחָד
2. אַתָּה מֹשֶׁה נוֹדֶה מוֹדֶה דוֹמֶה
3. שַׁבָּת שַׁבַּת שָׁבַת בַּשַּׁבָּת הַשַּׁבָּת
4. מִי כָּמֹכָה בַּקֹּדֶשׁ קָדוֹשׁ הַקָּדוֹשׁ
5. זֶה אֶל זֶה נָתַתָּ וָעֵד נָטַע בֵּינִי
6. אוֹת הִיא כִּי שֵׁשֶׁת תָּמִיד נֶפֶשׁ

8. The following words are all real Hebrew words. Read them aloud until you can read them easily.

1. פִּיו פִּיהָ פֹּה פֵּיוֹת פָּח פּוֹנֶה

2. נָפַל נֶפֶת נוֹפֵל נֶפֶשׁ סָפַק

3. צוֹק צוֹבָה צָדוֹק צַדִּיק צֶדֶק

4. קוֹל קוֹלִי קוֹלוֹ קוֹלָהּ קוֹלוֹת

5. שׁוֹאֵב שֹׁאֵל שֹׁכֵב שֶׁקֶל

6. תּוֹדָה תּוֹכוֹ תּוֹלַד תָּמִיד תַּחַת

7. אֵיפֹה אֵיפַת אָכוֹל אֹכֵל וָאֹכַל

8. בַּעַל בִּצָּה בָּצֵק בִּקֵּשׁ בַּיִת

9. גָּדוֹל גָּעַל דּוֹדִי דּוֹדָה כִּפָּה

10. הַבֵּט הֵבִיא הוֹד הוֹדִיעַ הִנֵּה

11. זֹאת זֶה זָכָה חָדַל חֶדֶק חֹדֶשׁ

12. מָצָא מוֹצֵא מֹצֵאת מֵצַח מַצָּה

Words from Our Tradition

month	=	חֹדֶשׁ	righteous	=	צַדִּיק
matza	=	מַצָּה	righteousness	=	צֶדֶק

skullcap, yarmulke = כִּפָּה

unit of Israeli money = שֶׁקֶל

Learning Hints and Suggestions

1. Sometimes a dot in Hebrew serves double duty. For example, the same dot can be both the dot on the letter שׁ and the vowel Xׄ. The most common example of this is the word for **Moses**, מֹשֶׁה. The dot above the letter שׁ is also the vowel Xׄ, pronounced after the letter מ.

2. Write your own English sentences with Hebrew letter and vowel combinations.

3. Using your flashcards, see how many English words you can spell in five minutes with the Hebrew letters and vowels that you have learned so far.

4. Now see how many of the words from #3 you can spell differently.

LESSON 7

ר שׁ שׂ ת

These are the letters and vowels you have already learned:

א בּ ב ג ד ה ו ז

ח ט י כּ כ ל מ

נ ס ע פּ פ צ ק שׁ ת

Xָ Xַ Xִ Xִי Xֵ Xֵי Xֶ Xוֹ Xֹ

In this lesson you will learn the end of the alphabet. The letter שׂ is very similar to the letter שׁ, which you have learned. The letter שׁ **SH** has a dot on the upper right side. The letter שׂ **S** has a dot on the upper left side.

R as in **R**obin	ר
SH as in **SH**ape **S** as in **S**un	שׁ שׂ
T as in **T**all	ת

Look-Alikes Notice the difference between the letters ד **D** and ר **R**. The letter ד has a projection in the upper right corner. The letter ר is rounded in the upper right corner.

Notice the difference between the letter שׁ **SH** and the letter שׂ **S**. שׁ **SH** has a dot over the upper right corner. שׂ **S** has a dot over the upper left corner.

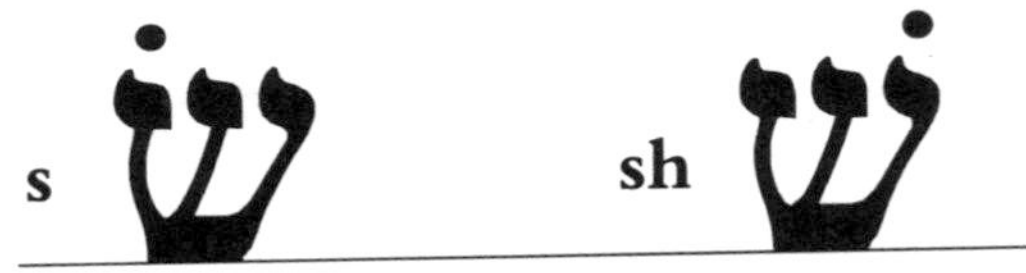

Sound-Alikes The letters שׂ and ס have the same sound.

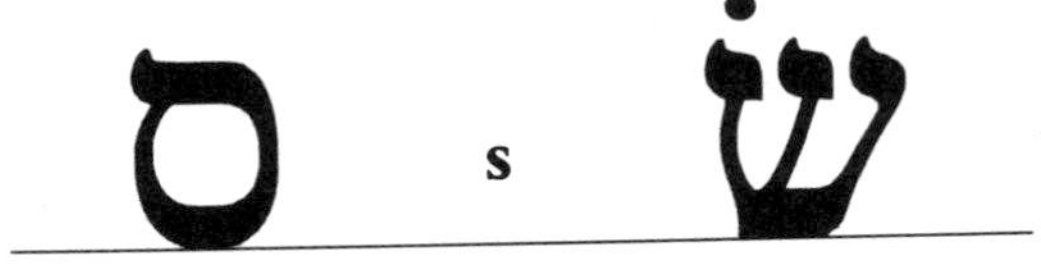

Read the following lines.

Vowels These are the vowels you have already learned:

Xֹ Xוֹ Xֶ Xֵי Xֵ Xִי Xִ Xַ Xָ

The vowel sound for this lesson is:

oo as in **zoo** Xֻ Xוּ

The vowel sound **oo** may be written as the letter ו with a dot in the middle וּ, appearing to the left of a Hebrew consonant.

זוּ = Xוּ + ז

zoo = oo + z

suit = סוּט pool = פּוּל

The vowel sound **oo** may also be written as three dots underneath a Hebrew consonant.

זֻ = Xֻ + ז

zoo = oo + z

suit = סֻט pool = פֻּל

Read the following lines aloud.

1. שׁוּ תוּ זוּ לוּ רוּ שׁוּ מוּ קוּ כּוּ

2. בֻּ דֻ גֻ עֻ טֻ יֻ צֻ סֻ אֻשׁ פֻּק

3. בּוּת רוּד קוּל חוּק מֻב פֻּז לֻט

Compare the uses of the letter ו.

Read the following lines aloud.

1. אוּ אוֹ אֶ וּבָ שׁוּ לֶ שֶׁל שׁוּל
2. שׁוּב וּמִי אֶב וּמַה וּפִי עוּת
3. פַּת פּוּת וּבוֹא וָבוּד וָבוֹא

Below is a chart showing how to write the Hebrew letters in this lesson.

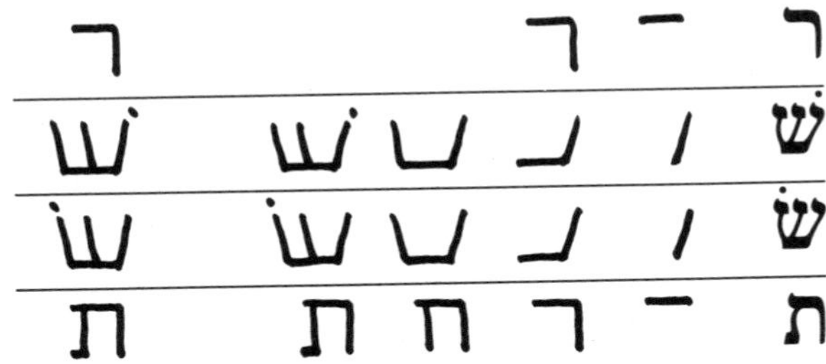

Exercises

1. Write one line of each new letter with each of the vowel sounds you have learned, sounding the letters with the vowels as you write them.

2. In the pair of lines below, match the printed letters with the block print letters.

3. Pronounce each letter in each line. Circle the letters that sound like the English letter in the box.

4. Circle the words that sound alike in each line.

1. רַק דָּק רִשׁ דּוֹשׁ רַב רָס רַת דַּאק
2. צוּר צוּד אוּר אֱד אֹד צֱד
3. שִׁיב סִיד סֵיו שִׁיר סֵיד שֵׁאב
4. קֹס כּוֹשׁ בּוֹשׁ כֹּט קֱשׁ כּוֹשׁ קוֹשׁ
5. עָשָׂה אָסָא עָשַׂא אַסַח אַטָת צָשַׂה

5. Spell each of the following words in as many ways as you can, using Hebrew letters.

1. root
2. cool
3. sofa
4. tool
5. soak
6. ooze
7. pizza
8. boot
9. lose
10. bore
11. tour
12. mess

6. Read the following prayerbook words and phrases.

1. גָּדוֹל הַגָּדוֹל הַגִּבּוֹר הַנּוֹרָא
2. עָלֵינוּ אָבִינוּ קוֹלֵנוּ עִמָּנוּ
3. אַתָּה אֶחָד מֹשֶׁה זֹאת הַתּוֹרָה
4. כִּי בּוֹ שָׁבַת מִכֹּל בָּרָא לָתֵת לוֹ
5. דּוֹר וָדוֹר עַל כֹּל הַחֶסֶד עָשִׂיתָ

7. Write the following dialogue using Hebrew letters and vowels. Betty said to Pa: "Tell Ma to get me a Teddy Bear. Tell Ma to read me a tale. Tell Ma to bake me a cake. Tell Ma to get me a red bed. Tell Ma to take me to a zoo. Tell Ma to take me to a new show." Pa said: "Not today! No Teddy Bear, no tale, no cake, no red bed, no zoo, no new show. Today, make your bed neat, eat your peas, obey your Ma. Behave today. Maybe tomorrow you may go."

8. The following words are all real Hebrew words. Read them aloud until you can read them easily.

1. אַדִּיר אָז אִירָא אֶפֶס אָרַב אֹמֵר
2. בָּשָׂר בֹּחֵר בֹּרֵא בַּיִת בַּעַל בֹּקֶר
3. דָּבָר דֶּבֶק דֹּבֶר דָּת דָּקַר דָּרַשׁ
4. הֶבֶל הֵידָד הָמָה הֶרֶב הַשָׂדֶה
5. וָלָד וָעֶד וָזָר וַיַּאת וָשֹׁד וָשֶׂה
6. שָׂדֶה שָׂדִי שֶׂה שָׂחַק שׂוֹרָה שָׂמַח
7. זֹאת זֶה זֵכֶר זֹכֵר זֶרַע זָרַק
8. וּבוֹא וּבוֹר וּמַהֵר וּמוּל וּפָּנָיו
9. סָגוּר סוֹד סַעַר סֵפֶר סָבִיב סֵדֶר
10. נוּסוּ נַחַת נֵר נֶצַח נָשִׂיא נִשָׂא

11. מֹשֶׁה מוֹשָׁב מוּשׁ מָהִיר מַזָּל

12. שַׁעַר שֵׂעָר שַׂק רֹאשׁ הַשָּׁנָה

13. כֻּלָּנוּ עֻזִּי סֻכּוֹת כֻּבַּד חֻקָּה חֻפָּה

14. תּוֹרָה תֵּבֵל תָּמַהּ תָּעָה תֻּמָּה תּוּר

15. כָּתוּב שָׁמוּר זָכוּר קָצוּר רָאוּ

16. פֻּעַל פֶּסַח פָּנִיתָ פֶּתַח פֶּשַׁע פֶּרַע

17. עָשִׂיתִי עָשׂוּ עֹשֶׂה שׁוּנִי שׁוּמָה

18. הִשָּׁמֵר וַיֹּאמֶר הָרָעוֹת תּוֹחֶלֶת

19. קֻצַּח שָׁלוֹשׁ שָׂנֵא שׂוֹנֵא שׁוֹסַע

20. עֶזֶר צִיצִת רֶשַׁע רַעַשׁ יָבֵשׁ

Words from Our Tradition

Succot = סֻכּוֹת Seder = סֵדֶר

Torah = תּוֹרָה Moses = מֹשֶׁה

Passover = פֶּסַח fortune, luck = מַזָּל

New Year = רֹאשׁ הַשָּׁנָה

Learning Hints and Suggestions

1. One way that may help you distinguish the sounds וֹ and וּ is to think of the letter ו as a little person.

• With an idea in his head (on top of the letter), he says:

oh! oh! וֹ וֹ

• With a pain in his stomach (in the middle of the letter), he says:

oo! oo! וּ וּ

2. Make up your own English sentences using only Hebrew letter sounds.

LESSON 8

These are the letters and vowels you have already learned:

Final Letters

Five Hebrew letters have a different form when they are written at the end of a word. The regular and final forms of a letter are still the same letter, and they are pronounced in the same way.

CH as in Ba**CH**	ך	כ
M as in **M**other	ם	מ
N as in **N**ow	ן	נ
F as in **F**ood	ף	פ
TS as in Nu**TS**	ץ	צ

1. The normal form of the letter כ **CH** as in Ba**CH** is used at the beginning and in the middle of words.

כָּמוֹכָה שָׁכַב

The final form ךְ **CH** as in Ba**CH** is only used at the end of words.

לָךְ אֵלֵךְ

Both כ and ךְ are pronounced **CH** as in Ba**CH**.

The final form ך is usually written with two dots inside it ךְ. These dots have no sound. Sometimes the vowel ָ appears inside the final form ךָ. This is pronounced **CHA**.

2. The normal form of the letter מ **M** as in **M**other is used at the beginning and in the middle of words.

מָצָא שׁוֹמֵר

The final form ם **M** as in **M**other is used only at the end of words.

אֵם בָּנִים

Both מ and ם are pronounced **M** as in **M**other.

3. The normal form of the letter נ **N** as in **N**ow is used at the beginning and in the middle of words.

נָטַע שָׁנָה

The final form ן **N** as in **N**ow is used only at the end of words.

בֵּן אָמֵן

Both נ and ן are pronounced **N** as in **N**ow.

4. The normal form of the letter **פ F** as in **F**ood is used at the beginning and in the middle of words.

נָפַל   שׁוֹפָר

The final form **ף F** as in **F**ood is used only at the end of words.

אַף   כָּנָף

Both **פ** and **ף** are pronounced **F** as in **F**ood.

5. The normal form of the letter **צ TS** as in nu**TS** is used at the beginning and in the middle of words.

צָבָא   רָצָה

The final form **ץ TS** as in nu**TS** is used only at the end of words.

אֶרֶץ   עֵץ

Both **צ** and **ץ** are pronounced **TS** as in nu**TS**.

Read the following lines.

1. כַּךְ בָּךְ בָּכָה לָךְ סִךְ עָלֶיךָ בֵּיתֵךְ

2. מִם מַיִם עִם עֶמֶק לָהֶם לֶחֶם הֶם

3. נֵן מִנָה בֶּן אֶדֶן הָמָן נֶדֶר נֵלֶךְ

4. פַּף פֶּרֶק דַּף כָּנָף אֶלֶף פּוּרִים

Look-Alikes Some final forms look like other Hebrew letters. The final form of the letter כ looks like the letter ד. The letter ךְ is longer than the letter ד, and has either two dots or the vowel ָ beside it.

Notice the difference between the final form ם **M** and the letter ס **S**. The final letter ם is square at the bottom. The letter ס is rounded at the bottom.

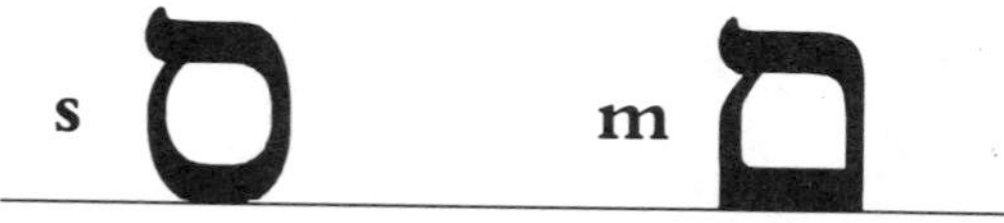

Notice the difference between the final form ן **N** and the letter ו **V**. The final letter ן extends below the line of the other letters. The letter ו does not.

Read the following lines aloud.

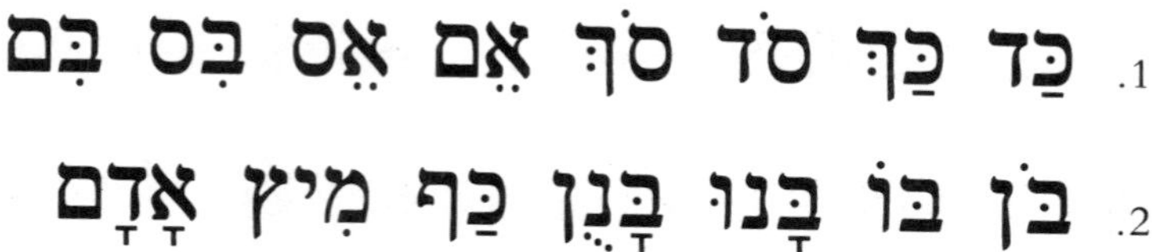

1. כַּד כַּךְ סֹד סֹךְ אֶם אֵס בִּס בִּם
2. בֹּן בּוֹ בָּנוּ בָּנֶן כַּף מִיץ אָדָם

Below is a chart showing how to write the final letters introduced in this lesson.

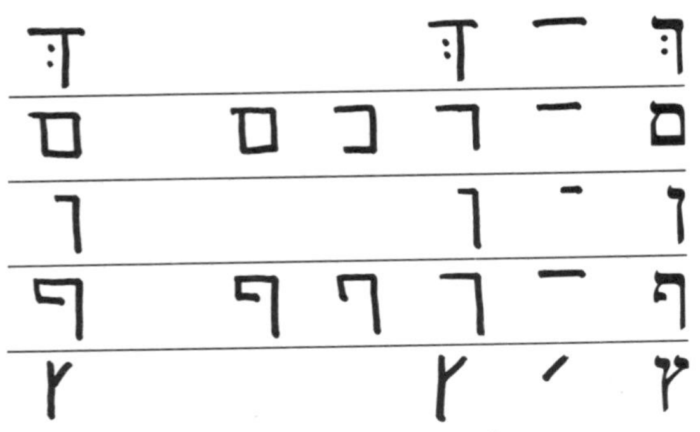

Exercises

1. Write one line each of the regular and final forms of the letters given above. Pronounce each form as you write.

2. In the pairs of lines below, match the printed letters with the block letters.

3. Pronounce each letter in each line. Circle the letters that sound like the English letter in the box.

N	נ ו ן ג ו נ ן ךְ
CH	כּ ה ח ךְ ד כ ח ה
M	מ ס ם מ ם ט מ ס
TS	צ ץ ע צ א ף ץ ע
F	פּ פ ץ ף פ ף כּ פּ
Silent	צ א ע ץ ע ף צ א

4. Write in the blanks the proper form of the letter shown at the beginning of each line.

1. נ ן _ָפַל עַיִ_ _ָתַתָּ אֵי_ בֵּי_
2. מ ם _ָגֵן אֵ_ _ֶלֶךְ _וֹצֶה עָרִי_
3. כ ךְ מֶלֶ_ בָּ_ָה הֹלֶ_ דֶרֶ_ שׁוֹ_ֵן
4. צ ץ _ֶדֶק אֶרֶ_ _ִיוֹן מַ_ָה עֵ_
5. פ ף סֵ_ֶר אָסַ_ רֹדֵ_ יָ_ֶה וּ_ַר

5. Read the names of the letters in the Hebrew alphabet aloud. They are listed in alphabetical order. The initial letter of each word will tell you which letter is being named. Write all the forms of all the letters in the Hebrew alphabet and copy the correct letter-name next to each one.

אָלֶף בֵּית גִּמֶל דָּלֶת הֵא וָו זַיִן חֵית

טֵית יוֹד כַּף לָמֶד מֵם נוּן סָמֶךְ עַיִן

פֵּא צָדִי קוֹף רֵישׁ שִׁין תָּו

6. Circle the words that sound alike in each line.

1. מָרוֹם מֹדִים מָנוּס מוֹדִם שָׁלוֹם
2. נֹתֵן גֹּאֵל גֶּפֶן גֹּנֵב נֹפֵל גּוֹנֵיו
3. יַחַד יוֹסֵד הוֹדוּ הָמוֹן יָכָד חָזָק
4. אֶרֶו צָבָא צָרָה עֶרֶב אֵצֶל עֹשֶׂה
5. רָצוֹן דֹּרוֹט דֶּרֶךְ דּוֹרוֹת רָשָׁע שֵׁם
6. סֵפֶר שָׂרָה שָׁמַר שָׂמַח שֵׂיפֶר
7. עֵף עֵצִים יוֹם יָמִים אֵיצִם עֵת
8. טוֹבִים כֹּל הֹלֵךְ לָכֶם לָהֵן קוֹל זֶה

7. Read the following prayerbook words and phrases.

1. אֶת שֵׁם הַמֶּלֶךְ הַגָּדוֹל הַגִּבּוֹר
2. קָדוֹשׁ הוּא כֻּלָּם שָׁמַיִם זֶה מִזֶּה
3. בָּרוּךְ מֶלֶךְ הָעוֹלָם יוֹצֵר אוֹר
4. וּבוֹרֵא חֹשֶׁךְ עֹשֶׂה שָׁלוֹם וּבוֹרֵא
5. אֶת הַכֹּל הַמֵּאִיר לָאָרֶץ עָלֶיהָ
6. עַמּוֹ תָּמִיד חָדָשׁ עַל צִיּוֹן תָּאִיר
7. בָּחַר בָּנוּ מִכָּל הָעַמִּים נָתַן
8. לָנוּ אֶת תּוֹרָתוֹ נוֹתֵן הַתּוֹרָה
9. נֵר שֶׁל שַׁבָּת עָנוּ שִׁירָה רַבָּה
10. מִי כָּמֹכָה בַּקֹּדֶשׁ עֹשֶׂה פֶּלֶא
11. כַּכָּתוּב עַל יָד מִפִּינוּ לֹא יָמוּשׁ
12. בֵּינִי אוֹת הִיא כִּי שֵׁשֶׁת יָמִים

8. The following words are all real Hebrew words. Read them aloud until you can read them easily.

1. אֶדֶן אֶלֶף אָדוֹם אֶרֶץ אָקוּם אַךְ
2. בָּנִים בָּרוּךְ בֶּגֶד בִּקֵשׁ בַּעַל בָּם
3. גַּן גָּדוֹל גֹּרֶן גֹּמֶל גַּם גֶּפֶן גַּד
4. דֶּרֶךְ דּוֹרוֹת דַּלִּים דָּמִים דָּרַשׁ
5. הוֹלֵךְ הָרָן הָרִים הֵן הָדַף הוּא
6. וַיֵּלֶךְ וַיָּקָם וַיֹּאמֶר וַיִּגַּשׁ וָלָד
7. זֶרַע זֵיתִים זוּלָתוֹ זִמֵּר זָמַם זָז
8. חֹרֶף חֵן חָמֵץ חַלָּה חָפֵץ חוּץ חָם
9. טָהוֹר טוֹבִים טַבַּעַת טָרוֹף טָמֵא
10. יוֹם יַיִן יוֹעֵץ יָשַׁב יוֹנָה יַךְ יָם
11. כֵּן כָּנָף כֶּסֶף כֹּהֵן כִּכָּר כֻּלּוֹ כַּף

12. לֶחֶם לָכֵן לֵוִי לֵבָב לָכֶם לָךְ לִי

13. מֶלֶךְ מָגֵן מַיִם מִן מָקוֹם מָשׂוֹשׂ

14. נָתַן נָשָׂא נָחָשׁ נִחָם נֶגֶף נִקָה נֵר

15. סוּר סָךְ סוּף סַפִּיר סֻכּוֹת סֵתֶר

16. עֵץ עִם עַיִן עֵרֶךְ עֶבֶד עֶצֶם

17. פֶּרֶץ פָּנַיִךְ פִּקּוּד פַּעם פּוּרִים

18. צִיּוֹן צָפוֹן צָרָה צֹאן צֶלֶם צוֹרֵף

19. קֶדֶם קוּם קָטֹן קִבּוּץ קַיִן קַו

20. רָחַץ רֶחֶם רַבִּים רַע רֹאשׁ רָם

21. שֵׂךְ שָׂרַף שָׂנֵא שִׂים שָׂחַק שֵׂעִיר

22. שֹׁאֵל שָׁאַן שָׁבָץ שַׁדִין שָׁוֵה שׁוּף

23. תֹּרֶן תֹּקֶף תָּמִים תּוֹךְ תּוֹדָה

Words from Our Tradition

yes	=	כֵּן	blessed	=	בָּרוּךְ
king	=	מֶלֶךְ	big	=	גָּדוֹל
tree	=	עֵץ	vine	=	גֶּפֶן
Zion	=	צִיּוֹן	wine	=	יַיִן

Learning Hints and Suggestions

1. You have now learned all the letters of the Hebrew alphabet. It is very important that you continue to review your flashcards, to reinforce your learning and improve your understanding of letters that are difficult for you.

2. You have now learned all the letters and final letters. Here is a useful additional activity at this point: open your prayerbook to any page. Pronounce each letter on that page, disregarding vowels and word divisions. Just say the sound of each letter as you go. The repetition involved in this exercise will greatly improve your ability to recognize letters. You will not yet be able to read all the words, but you should be able to read about half of them. After you have pronounced several lines of individual letters, go back and read as many whole words as you can. If possible, do this exercise every day.

3. See if you can find someone in your community who can read Hebrew. Check your synagogue, Jewish Community Center, or college/university. Read a few of the exercises in this book, and have the person check your pronunciation of Hebrew letters and vowels.

LESSON 9

THE SHEVA

These are the vowels you have already learned:

Xֻ וּX Xֹ וֹX Xֶ יXֵ Xֵ יXִ Xִ Xַ Xָ

The vowel for this lesson is called the **sheva.**

silent/short-sound Xְ

Each of the vowels you have learned so far is always pronounced with a single sound. The sheva is sometimes silent, and sometimes pronounced with a short, slurred sound, like the **e** in stup**e**fy.

The Sheva at the Beginning of a Word A sheva at the beginning of a Hebrew word is always pronounced with a short, slurred sound.

maroon = מְרוֹן   lagoon = לְגוֹן

Read the following line aloud.

דְּבַר כְּתַב שְׁמַע מְחַל כְּלַל סְלַח

The Sheva at the End of a Word A sheva at the end of a word is always a silent vowel, and it is not pronounced at all. You have already seen this under the final form of the letter ךְ.

shot = שָׁתְ Bach = בָּךְ

Read the following line aloud.

לָךְ אַתְ חָרַתְ אֱלֶךְ מַתְ מִמֵּךְ

The Sheva in the Middle of a Word Whenever two shevas appear side by side in the middle of a word, the first sheva is silent, and the second is pronounced with the short, slurred sound.

consummate = קַנְסְמֵית

Read the following line aloud.

תִּשְׁמְרוּ תִּכְתְּבִי יִזְכְּרוּ יִשְׁלְחוּ

When a sheva appears alone in the middle of a word, it is usually silent. Without an understanding of Hebrew grammar, it is difficult to know when a sheva in the middle of a word is silent and when it is pronounced. We suggest that you not pronounce a sheva when it appears alone in the middle of a word, although this is not always exactly correct.

concave = קַנְקֵב carpool = כַּרְפּוּל

Read the following lines aloud. Each sheva is a silent vowel.

1. יִזְכֹּר יִכְתֹּב יִשְׁמֹר יִפְקֹד יִמְלֹךְ

2. דַּלְתִּי דַּרְכִּי אַרְצִי רַגְלִי סַלְעִי

3. מַלְכֵי כַּנְפֵי אַנְשֵׁי עַבְדֵי חַסְדֵי

Read the following lines aloud. Each sheva in these lines must be pronounced with the short, slurred sound.

1. פְּרִי שְׁמִי בְּנֵי לְכִי בְּלִי שְׁבִי

2. קְדוֹשׁ מְלֹא מְלֹךְ שְׁמֹר יְסוֹד

3. וְאוֹר וְגָד וְדוֹר וְהוּא וְזֶה וְזֹאת

4. גְּדוֹלָה כְּתוּבָה קְדוֹשָׁה שְׁבוּעַ

Read the following lines aloud. In each word, the first sheva is silent, and the second sheva is pronounced with the short, slurred sound.

1. יִשְׁפְּטוּ תִּמְצְאוּ שִׁבְתְּךָ תִּבְטְחוּ

2. תִּשְׁמְעוּ מִשְׁפְּחוֹת חַסְדְּךָ

Combination Vowels

The sheva is sometimes written under a letter along with another vowel.

When sheva appears next to the vowel אַ or the vowel אֶ, it is silent, and pronunciation of the vowel does not change.

a as in y**a**cht = אַ = אֲ

odd = עַד = עֲד

eh as in b**e**d = אֶ = אֱ

Ed = עֶד = עֱד

When a sheva appears next to the vowel אָ, the pronunciation changes to **o** as in l**o**w.

o as in l**o**w = אֹ = אֳ

ode = עֹד = עֳד

Read the following lines aloud.

1. אֲדוֹן עֲשֶׂה עֲדִי הֲמוֹן חֲנִית הֲדַס
2. אֱדֹם אֱמֶת אֱלִיל אֱנוֹשׁ אֶעֱשֶׂה
3. עֳנִי אֳנִי צִפֳּרִים שִׁבֳּלִים
4. רַחֲמִים אֲנָשִׁים תֶּאֱרֹב אֲנִי

Sheva Summary The chart below shows when the sheva is silent, and when it has the short-sound.

SILENT

at the end of a word — אַתְ

the first of two in a row — יִשְׁמְרוּ

alone in the middle of a word — מַלְכֵי

next to the vowels Xֶ and Xַ — אֱמֶת, אֲשֶׁר

SHORT-SOUND

at the beginning of a word — דְּבַר

the second of two in a row — יִשְׁמְרוּ

SOUND CHANGE

next to the vowel Xָ (from **a** to **o**) — עֳנִי

Exercises

1. Write each letter of the Hebrew alphabet with each of the vowels you know. Pronounce each letter and vowel as you write. If you are having difficulty with any of the letters or vowels, review some of the earlier exercises in this book until you feel comfortable with them.

2. Write the following English words using Hebrew letters and vowels. Each word should include a sheva.

1. beanpole	3. sedate	5. cologne
2. marine	4. parade	6. Tuesday

3. Circle the words that sound alike in each line.

1. זָקְנוּ נָסְעוּ קָרְאוּ נָשְׂאוּ אָמְרוּ
2. אֶקְרָא אַנְשֵׁי עַפְכֹּד עָזְרָה אַפְקִיד
3. תַּכְלִית תִּשְׁמֹר טָחְלִת תִּכְתֹּב
4. בְּרִית בְּבֵית בַּרְכוֹ בְּוֹט בְּנֵי בְּנוֹת
5. שָׁמְרָה סְלַח שַׁמְתִּי שְׁמַע שְׁלָךְ
6. יִרְעַא יִצְחָק יִרְאָה יֵדְעוּ יְקָר
7. מְנָת מִשְׂרָה מָצְאוּ מִצְוָה מִצְבַּע
8. אֲנִי אֲשֶׁר אֲבוֹת אֱמֶת עֲבוֹט אֲחִי
9. שָׁמַע שָׁמַר שָׁבַח שָׁכַח שָׁנַךְ
10. רָץ רָאָה דָּף רָצָה דָּק רָעָה
11. אֶפְקֹד אֶפָּקֵד אֲפַקֵּד אֶפָּקֵד
12. בְּנֵךְ בִּנְךָ בָּנַיִךְ בְּנֶךָ בְּנֵךְ

4. Add a sheva to every consonant below that does not have a vowel. Read each word aloud.

1. גּדוֹלָה בּרִית זמַן נשָׁמָה צדָקָה
2. שׁוֹמרִים זֹכרִים הֹלכִים מַלכוּת
3. כּתבוּ נָסעוּ יָשׁבוּ שָׁפטוּ גָּנבוּ
4. אֶפקֹד אֶלמַד תִּרכַּב יִזכֹּר נִדבַּק
5. כּתֹב מלֹךְ שׁמַע שׁלַח פּתַח קצֹר
6. מִשׁכָּב לִפנֵי מִדבַּר מִשׁכָּן מִנחָה

5. Below is a group of Hebrew words from our tradition. You may know some or all of them. The translations are on page 92.

1. שְׁמַע
2. יִשְׂרָאֵל
3. מְזוּזָה
4. מְנוֹרָה
5. בְּרָכָה
6. צְדָקָה
7. יְרוּשָׁלַיִם
8. לְחַיִּים
9. אַבְרָהָם
10. יִצְחָק
11. יַעֲקֹב
12. מִצְוָה
13. שִׂמְחָה
14. תְּפִלָּה
15. חֲנוּכָּה

6. Read the following excerpts from well-known prayers.

1. שִׂים שָׁלוֹם, טוֹבָה וּבְרָכָה, חֵן
וָחֶסֶד וְרַחֲמִים, עָלֵינוּ וְעַל כָּל
יִשְׂרָאֵל עַמֶּךָ. בָּרְכֵנוּ אָבִינוּ,
כֻּלָּנוּ כְּאֶחָד, בְּאוֹר פָּנֶיךָ.

2. יִתְבָּרַךְ וְיִשְׁתַּבַּח, וְיִתְפָּאַר
וְיִתְרוֹמַם, וְיִתְנַשֵּׂא וְיִתְהַדַּר

3. שִׁירָה חֲדָשָׁה שִׁבְּחוּ גְאוּלִים
לְשִׁמְךָ עַל שְׂפַת הַיָּם: יַחַד כֻּלָּם
הוֹדוּ וְהִמְלִיכוּ וְאָמְרוּ

4. וְקוֹנֵה הַכֹּל, וְזוֹכֵר חַסְדֵי אָבוֹת,
וּמֵבִיא גוֹאֵל לִבְנֵי בְנֵיהֶם

5. וְשָׁמְרוּ בְנֵי יִשְׂרָאֵל אֶת הַשַּׁבָּת

7. The following words are all real Hebrew words. Read them aloud until you can read them easily.

1. אֲדָמָה אַהֲבָה אֱמֶת אֲנַחְנוּ אַתְּ
2. בְּרָכָה בְּטֶרֶם בְּלִי בָּרְכוּ בְּבַיִת
3. גְּאֻלָּה גָּדְלֵךְ גְּוִיָּה גְּנֹב גָּמַרְתִּי
4. דְּבָרִים דַּרְכֵי דְּבוֹרָה דְּרָשָׁה
5. הִמְלִיכוּ הָלְכָה הֲלִיכוֹת הֲלֹם
6. וְלֵךְ וְדָבָר וְאֵלֵךְ וְזֶה וְאֶחָד
7. זָכַרְתִּי זִלְפָּה זְמַן זֵדִים זְקֵנָה
8. חֲדָשָׁה חֵטְא חֲסָדִים חֶבְלֵי חֶפְצוֹ
9. טְהוֹרָה טַעְמוֹ טַפְּכֶם טוֹפְלֵי טוֹב
10. יְדַבֵּר יַעֲקֹב יִשְׂרָאֵל יְהוּדָה יִצְחָק
11. כְּתַבְתֶּם כַּאֲשֶׁר כְּתֻבָּה כֹּהֲנִים
12. לִפְנֵי לְהַדְלִיק לְבָרֵךְ לְעוֹלָם וָעֶד

13. מַעֲשֶׂה מִצְוָה מִשְׁפָּחָה מְאֹדֶךָ

14. נֶאֱמַר נֶאֱמָן נְשָׁמָה נְבִיאִים נָעֳמִי

15. סְלַח סְפָרִים סִיסְרָא סַנְחֵרִיב

16. עֶלְיוֹן עֲרָבִים עֲבָדִים עֶזְרָה

17. פְּרִי פְּנֵי פְּלִישְׁתִּים פְּעָמִים

18. צְדָקָה צְבָאוֹת יָצִיץ צַלְמָוֶת

19. קִדְּשָׁנוּ קְדוֹשָׁה קְרוֹבִים קַשְׁתּוֹ

20. רַחֲמִים רִבְקָה רְשָׁעִים רַגְלֵינוּ

21. שׁוֹמְרֵי שְׁבִיעִי שְׁכִינָה שֶׁלְּךָ

22. שְׂרָפִים שִׂמְחָה שְׂדֵי שׂוֹנְאֵי

23. תִּפְאֶרֶת תְּהִלָּה תַּלְמוּד תְּשׁוּבָה

24. אַדִּיר בּוֹאֲכֶם גּוֹמֵל הַמְבֹרָךְ

25. חֵלֶק טֹטָפֹת יְצִיר כִּכְלוֹת נַקְדִּישׁ

Synagogue Vocabulary

The following words are associated with synagogue life.

Torah = תּוֹרָה

pulpit = בִּימָה

siddur = סִדּוּר

cantor = חַזָּן

rabbi = רָב

menorah = מְנוֹרָה

yarmulke = כִּפָּה

tefillin = תְּפִילִין

tallit = טַלִּית

shofar = שׁוֹפָר

eternal light = נֵר תָּמִיד

ark with Torah = אֲרוֹן הַקֹּדֶשׁ

pointer for the Torah = יָד

Bar Mitzvah = בַּר מִצְוָה

Bat Mitzvah = בַּת מִצְוָה

Learning Hints and Suggestions

By now you have learned enough to be able to read just about everything in the prayerbook. In the next lesson you will have some additional practice, and will learn about a few oddities and exceptions to what you have learned.

1. Open a Hebrew prayerbook and start reading! The more you read, the easier it will be for you. Feel free to go back and review any letters or vowels you are having trouble with.

2. Go to synagogue services. This is a great way to reinforce what you have learned, by listening to others and following along.

LESSON 10

LONG WORDS AND UNUSUAL ENDINGS

You have now learned all the Hebrew letters and vowels. To review, see charts inside the front and back covers. In this lesson, you will learn to read longer Hebrew words by breaking them into syllables.

Syllables A Hebrew syllable almost always begins with a consonant. It consists of either:

1. A consonant plus a vowel:

שַׁ בָּ מִי דֵּי קוֹ

2. A consonant plus a vowel plus another consonant:

שַׁל בָּא מִית דֵּיר קוֹב

Read the following examples of long words broken into syllables.

יִשְׂ + רָ + אֵל = יִשְׂרָאֵל

יְ + רוּ + שָׁ + לַ + יִם = יְרוּשָׁלַיִם

Here are more examples of words broken into syllables. Pronounce each word carefully.

1. וְ + דִ + בַּרְ + תָּ = וְדִבַּרְתָּ

2. שְׁ + כִי + נָ + תוֹ = שְׁכִינָתוֹ

3. וַ + אֲ + נַחְ + נוּ = וַאֲנַחְנוּ

Syllables and the Sheva In the last lesson, you learned that the sheva can be silent, or it can be pronounced with a short, slurred sound. When the sheva appears at the beginning of a word, it is a syllable by itself.

לְ + הַדְ + לִיק = לְהַדְלִיק

When two shevas appear in a row, the second is a syllable by itself.

מִשְׁ + פְּ + חוֹת = מִשְׁפְּחוֹת

In most other cases, a sheva indicates the end of a syllable.

A Note on Pronunciation Hebrew words are normally pronounced with the accent on the last syllable. Some words are pronounced with the accent on the second-to-last syllable. Without a knowledge of Hebrew grammar, it is not possible to be sure where to put the accent on a Hebrew word. When in doubt, put the accent at the end of the word. You will be correct most of the time. In many Hebrew prayerbooks, words that are not pronounced with the accent on the last syllable are shown with an accent mark: X֫. For example the word הָאֵ֫לֶּה is pronounced with the accent on the next to the last syllable.

Unusual Endings When the last letter of a word is ח, and the vowel underneath it is X̱, the combination is pronounced **ach**, and not **cha**.

roo-ach = רוּחַ ko-ach = כֹּחַ

נֹחַ שַׁבֵּחַ שַׂמֵּחַ מָשִׁיחַ שָׁלִיחַ סוֹלֵחַ

When the last vowel of a word is X̱ followed by the letter י, the combination X̱י is pronounced **I** as in **tie**.

my = מַי bowtie = בֹּתַי

עָלַי חַי בָּנַי אֲבוֹתַי אֲזַי דַי עֵינַי

Some Unusual Words There are a few common words in the prayerbook that are exceptions to the rules of pronunciation you have learned in this book.

The Word כָּל Although כָּל is spelled with the vowel Xָ, it is pronounced as if it were spelled כֹּל. The most well-known example is the opening prayer of the Yom Kippur service, Kol Nidre.

כָּל נִדְרֵי . . .

The Word מִצְוֹת The word מִצְוֹת is pronounced **mitsvot**. The word מִצְוֹתָיו is pronounced **mitsvotav**. See the note on page 88.

The Word צִוָּנוּ The word צִוָּנוּ is pronounced **tsivanu**. See the note on page 88.

The words מִצְוֹתָיו and צִוָּנוּ are found in many blessings.

אֲשֶׁר קִדְּשָׁנוּ בְּמִצְוֹתָיו וְצִוָּנוּ

Exercises

1. Read the following lines aloud. Each line builds up a long Hebrew word syllable by syllable. Pronounce each word several times until you can read it easily.

1. שֶׁ + הֶ, שֶׁהֶ + חֱ, שֶׁהֶחֱ + יָ,
שֶׁהֶחֱיָ + נוּ, שֶׁהֶחֱיָנוּ

2. וְ + קִ, וְקִ + יְּ, וְקִיְּ + מָ,
וְקִיְּמָ + נוּ, וְקִיְּמָנוּ

3. וְ + הִ, וְהִ + גִּי, וְהִגִּי + עָ,
וְהִגִּיעָ + נוּ, וְהִגִּיעָנוּ

4. וַ + אֲ, וַאֲ + נַחְ, וַאֲנַחְ + נוּ,
וַאֲנַחְנוּ

5. וּ + מִשְׁ, וּמִשְׁ + תַּ, וּמִשְׁתַּ + חֲ,
וּמִשְׁתַּחֲ + וִים, וּמִשְׁתַּחֲוִים

6. יְ + הַ, יְהַ + לֲ, יְהַלֲ + לוּ,
יְהַלֲלוּ + ךָ, יְהַלֲלוּךָ

2. Below are some more examples of long words divided into syllables. Pronounce each word several times until you can say it easily.

1. שִׁ + נַּנְ + תָּם = שִׁנַּנְתָּם
2. הַ + מִּתְ + נַ + שֵּׂא = הַמִּתְנַשֵּׂא
3. רַ + חֲ + מִים = רַחֲמִים
4. שֶׁ + מַּקְ + דִּי + שִׁים = שֶׁמַּקְדִּישִׁים
5. בְּ + תוֹ + רָ + תֶ + ךָ = בְּתוֹרָתֶךָ
6. מְ + קַ + דֵּשׁ = מְקַדֵּשׁ
7. וְ + שַׂמְּ + חֵ + נוּ = וְשַׂמְּחֵנוּ
8. וְ + קַלְ + קֵל = וְקַלְקֵל
9. מִשְׁ + פְּ + טֵי = מִשְׁפְּטֵי
10. יִשְׁ + מְ + רֶ + ךָ = יִשְׁמְרֶךָ
11. בְּ + שָׁכְ + בְּ + ךָ = בְּשָׁכְבְּךָ
12. מִשְׁ + תַּ + חֲ + וִים = מִשְׁתַּחֲוִים

3. In each line below, a long word has been broken into syllables. Read the syllables, and write the word in its complete form. Read the complete word several times.

1. וְ + תִמְ + לוֹךְ
2. הַשְׁ + מִ + עֵ + נוּ
3. תִפְ + אַרְ + תֵּךְ
4. צִדְ + קָתְ + ךָ
5. כְּ + מִגְ + דָּ + לוֹת

4. Divide the following words into syllables.
Examples:

אַשְׁ/רֵי/ךָ   וּ/מוֹ/שִׁי/עַ

1. הָעֲבוֹדָה וַעֲטֶרֶת הַשָּׁמַיִם אֱלִילִים
2. בַּעֲגָלָא נֶחֱמָטָא הוֹשִׁיעֵנוּ
3. יַמְלִיךְ יִתְגַּדַּל שֶׁיִּשְׁמַע מַשְׁבִּיעַ
4. תַּלְמִידִים אַבְרָהָם בִּשְׁמֵי אֶשְׁמַע

5. The Kaddish prayer is probably the most used prayer in all of Jewish life. It is said at the end of the various sections of the traditional service, and as a mourning prayer at the end of a life. Read aloud until you can read it easily. The translation can be found on page 88.

יִתְגַּדַּל וְיִתְקַדַּשׁ שְׁמֵהּ רַבָּא בְּעָלְמָא

דִּי בְרָא כִרְעוּתֵהּ, וְיַמְלִיךְ מַלְכוּתֵהּ

בְּחַיֵּיכוֹן וּבְיוֹמֵיכוֹן, וּבְחַיֵּי דְכָל

בֵּית יִשְׂרָאֵל, בַּעֲגָלָא וּבִזְמַן

קָרִיב, וְאִמְרוּ אָמֵן.

יְהֵא שְׁמֵהּ רַבָּא מְבָרַךְ לְעָלַם

וּלְעָלְמֵי עָלְמַיָּא.

יִתְבָּרַךְ וְיִשְׁתַּבַּח, וְיִתְפָּאַר וְיִתְרוֹמַם,

וְיִתְנַשֵּׂא וְיִתְהַדַּר, וְיִתְעַלֶּה וְיִתְהַלַּל

שְׁמֵהּ דְּקֻדְשָׁא, בְּרִיךְ הוּא, לְעֵלָּא

מִן כָּל בִּרְכָתָא וְשִׁירָתָא,

תֻּשְׁבְּחָתָא וְנֶחֱמָתָא, דַּאֲמִירָן

בְּעָלְמָא, וְאִמְרוּ אָמֵן.

יְהֵא שְׁלָמָא רַבָּא מִן שְׁמַיָּא, וְחַיִּים,

עָלֵינוּ וְעַל כָּל יִשְׂרָאֵל,

וְאִמְרוּ אָמֵן.

עֹשֶׂה שָׁלוֹם בִּמְרוֹמָיו, הוּא יַעֲשֶׂה

שָׁלוֹם עָלֵינוּ וְעַל כָּל יִשְׂרָאֵל,

וְאִמְרוּ אָמֵן.

If you can master this prayer, there will be no Hebrew with vowels that will be too difficult for you.

Here is the translation of the Kaddish, given in Hebrew on the two preceding pages.

"Glorified and sanctified be God's great name throughout the world which he has created according to his will. May he establish his kingdom in your lifetime and during your days, and within the life of the entire house of Israel, speedily and soon; and say, Amen.

"May his great name be blessed forever and to all eternity.

"Blessed and praised, glorified and exalted, extolled and honored, adored and lauded be the name of the Holy One, blessed be he, beyond all the blessings and hymns, praises and consolations that are ever spoken in the world; and say, Amen.

"May there be abundant peace from heaven, and life, for us and for all Israel; and say, Amen.

"He who creates peace in his celestial heights, may he create peace for us and for all Israel; and say, Amen."

Daily Prayer Book, Philip Birnbaum, 1977, p. 124.

The Word מִצְוֹת The word מִצְוֹת is a little confusing to read. The letter ו is pronounced as the consonant **v**, and the dot above it is the vowel **o**. Before the invention of printing, this word was written in a way that was easier to read: מִצְוֹת. When the printing press came along, the dot was moved to the top of the וֹ for a reason that is unknown today. This leaves us with the confusing word מִצְוֹת.

The Word צִוָּנוּ The letter ו in this word looks confusing. It has a vowel under it, but there is also a dot in it. In this word, the dot in the ו does not mean that it is the vowel **oo**. The dot has to do with Hebrew grammar, and not with pronunciation. Whenever you see a ו with a dot inside and a vowel underneath, pronounce the letter with the vowel underneath, and ignore the dot.

Suggestions for Further Study

You have now gained the ability to read Hebrew words. Congratulations! There are several options open to you now.

1. You can simply enjoy the sounds and rhythms of Hebrew, at home or in the synagogue. With practice, you will become more and more comfortable with reading this beautiful language.

2. You may have been captivated by what you have learned so far, and wish to learn more about the Hebrew of the prayerbook. If so, there is no better course of study available than the book *Prayerbook Hebrew the Easy Way,* available from EKS Publishing Company. This book will teach you the basic structures and meanings of the Hebrew language, in a way specially designed for people who want to read and understand Hebrew prayers. All vocabulary words are common prayerbook words. At the end of each chapter, a well-known Hebrew prayer is given to illustrate the concepts learned.

3. For those who want a more thorough introduction to Hebrew we recommend *The First Hebrew Primer for Adults,* also available from EKS Publishing Company. This covers all the basics of Hebrew grammar, focusing on the Hebrew Bible. Explanations are clear and simple, but more study is required than with *Prayerbook Hebrew the Easy Way.*

4. After completing this book, you are also ready to begin the study of modern Hebrew. There are a large number of books available for this purpose. Check your bookstore, community center, college or university.

ANSWERS TO EXERCISES

LESSON 1

Exercise 4, page 7

1. בָּב; בַּב
2. תָּת; תַּת
3. שָׁת; שַׁת

LESSON 2

Exercise 5, page 13

תגד ת דש ש בא. . .

Exercise 6, page 13 (Some of these words may be spelled in other ways.)

1. בִּת בִּית
2. דָּת דַּת
3. תִּיא תִּי
4. שִׁיא שִׁי
5. תִּיבִי תִּבִי תִּבִיא
6. שִׁת שִׁית
7. תָּת
8. אִית אִת
9. גָּת
10. שָׁת
11. אִיב אִב
12. אַד
13. שַׁא
14. דִּיד דִּד
15. בִּיד בִּד
16. בַּב

LESSON 3

Exercise 2, page 19

1. הָט
2. אִיט
3. הֵז
4. שֵׁיו
5. אֵיד
6. טִיא
7. אֵיט
8. בִּיא
9. בֵּית
10. הֵט
11. שֵׁד
12. וֵג

Exercise 3, page 20

H: ה; ה
T: ט; ת; ת; ט
CH: ח; ח
Z: ז; ז; ז
V: ו; ו; ו; ב

LESSON 3 (continued)

Exercise 5, page 21

1. בִּיט בֵּיט בְּהֵב
2. גֵּיב גֵּיז דֵּיב שֵׁיב שֵׁיו
3. בִּיד
4. גֵּית הֵיט דֵּית
5. שִׁיט שָׁת שֵׁדִי

Exercise 6, page 21

1. אַבִיב אָבִיו
2. אַתָּה אָטָ
3. הַבֵּת הַבֵּט
4. חִיט חִית
5. הַדִּישׁ הַדִּשׁ
6. הֵית הֵיט

Exercise 7, page 22

1. וטוב ו ה הדב הזה. . .
2. ה ה ה טוב שבת אח ג חד.

LESSON 4

Exercise 3, page 28

Y: י; י
K: כּ; כּ
CH: ח; כ; כ
M: מ; מ; מ
T: ת; ט; ת; ט
H: ל; ל
H: ה; ה

Exercise 4, page 28

1. טַדִי בָּדִי
2. כֵּיל טֵיל הֵיל דֵּיל
3. לֵזִי דֵּזִי מֵבִי כֵּתִי
4. מַמִי

Exercise 5, page 29 (Some of these words may be spelled in other ways.)

1. מֵט מֵית מֵת מֵיט
2. מֵז מֵיז
3. טֵיל תֵּל
4. גֵּת גֵּיט
5. כֵּיב כֵּיו כֵּב כֵּו
6. מִי מִא מִיא
7. שֵׁד שֵׁיד
8. הָת הַט
9. הִיט הִת הִית
10. לִיו לִב לִיב לִו
11. לֵת לֵיט לֵט לֵית
12. כַּת כָּט

LESSON 4 (continued)

Exercise 6, page 29

1. וַה בָא וָא אָו אָב
2. בִּיו בִּב
3. לַחַח לָכַח
4. אַוַל אָבַל
5. תָּמְשׁ טָמְשׁ
6. זָת זַט
7. בֵּייב בֵּיו
8. לִישׁ לְשׁ
9. מֵיטִי מֵתִי
10. וֵייו וֵייב

Exercise 7, page 30

משה וב י יש אל ל   ו שי ה
בשמחה בה; ואמ ו כל :
מי כמכה באלי . . .

LESSON 5

Exercise 3, page 35

Silent: א; ע; ע; א
S: ס; ס; ס
N: נ; נ
Y: י; י; י
M: מ; מ
D: ד; ד

Exercise 4, page 36 (Some of these words may be spelled in other ways.)

1. סִיד סְד
2. דִיל דְל
3. דֵית דֵט
4. יֵס
5. לֶת לֶט
6. נֶת נֶט
7. נְס נִיס
8. לְב לְו לִיב לִיו
9. יֶט יֶת
10. לִיס לְס
11. מֶשׁ
12. נִיט נִית נְת נְט

Exercise 5, page 36

1. סָבִיב סַוִיו
2. אֵית אֵיט אֶת עֶת אֶת
3. נֶטֶה נִיתֶע
4. עֶבֶד אֶוֶד

Exercise 6, page 36

See Betty eat.
Eat, Betty, eat.
See Betty eat quiche.
Eat quiche, Betty, eat quiche.
See Bob eat Betty's quiche.
See Betty beat Bob.

LESSON 6

Exercise 3, page 44

H: הּ; ה; ה
K: כּ; ק; ק
P: פּ; פּ
TS: צ; צ
F: פ; פ
V: ו; ב; ו
Silent: א; ע; א

LESSON 6 (continued)

Exercise 4, page 45 (Some of these words may be spelled in other ways.)

1. לוֹא לֹא לֹע לוֹע
2. פָּת פַּט
3. גוֹל גֹל
4. פֹּל פּוֹל
5. שׁוֹא שֹׁא שׁוֹע שֹׁע
6. פֹּק פּוֹק
7. מָצָה מַצַא
8. פִּיצָה פְּצָה פִּיצָא פְּצַא
9. קוֹקָה-קוֹלָה; כֹּכָה-כֹּלָה
10. כִּיז קִז קִיז כִּז

Exercise 5, page 45

1. פִּיט פְּת
2. הִפּוֹא הִיפֹּה
3. אֶצֹת עֶצוֹט
4. כִּיפָּה קִפַּע
5. אוֹכֶל עוֹחֶל
6. קֵטֵב כַּתֵיו
7. תֵּכַל טֵכַל
8. תְּדַל טִידַל
9. קִוָא כִּיוַ
10. פּוֹ פֹּא פֹּה; פֹּת פּוֹט

Exercise 6, page 46

Ma said: "He's a meany."
Pa said: "No! He's not a meany. He made a neat boat. He made a yacht. He gave me a TV. He gave me dough. Oh no! He's not a meany."

LESSON 7

Exercise 3, page 53

R: ר; ר
S: ס; שׂ; ס
T: ט; ת; ט
F: פ; פ
M: מ
K: ק; כ; ק; ק
V: ו; ב; ו

Exercise 4, page 54

1. דָק דַאק
2. צוּד צֻד
3. סֵיו שֵׂאב
4. קֹס כּוּשׁ
5. עָשָׂה אָסָא

Exercise 5, page 54 (Some of these words may be spelled in more than one way.)

1. רֻט רֻת רוּט רוּת
2. כֻּל קֻל כּוּל קוּל
3. סֹפָּה שֹׂפָּה סוֹפַּע שׂוֹפַּא
4. טוּל תוּל טֻל תֻל
5. שׂוֹק סֹק סוֹק שֹׂק

LESSON 7 (continued)

Exercise 5, page 54 (continued)

6. עֶז אֶז אוּז עוּז
7. פִּיצָה פְּצַע פִּיצָא
8. בּוּט בּוּת בֶּט בֶּת
9. לֶז לוּז
10. בּוֹר בֹּר
11. טוּר תֶּר תּוּר טֶר
12. מֶס מֶשׁ

Exercise 7, page 55 (The following is one of many ways to write this dialogue.)

בֶּתִי סֶד תוּ פָּה: ״תֶּל מַה תּוּ גֶּט
מִי אֵי תֶּדִי בֵּיר. תֶּל מַה תּוּ
רֵיד מִי אֵי טֵיל. תֶּל מַה תּוּ בֵּיק
מִי אֵי קֵק. תֶּל מַה תּוּ גֶּט מִי
אֵי רֶד בֶּד. תֶּל מַה תּוּ תֵּק מִי תּוּ
אֵי זוּ. תֶּל מַה תּוּ תֵּק מִי
תּוּ אֵי נוּ שׁוֹא.״
פָּה סֶד: ״נַת תּוּדֵי! נוֹ תֶּדִי בֵּיר,
נוֹ טֵיל, נוֹ קֵק, נוֹ רֶד
בֶּד, נוֹ זוּ, נוֹ נוּ שׁוֹא. תּוּדֵי,
מֵק יוּר בֶּד נַיִת, אִיט יוּר
פִּיז, אוֹבֵּי יוּר מָה. בִּהֵיב תּוּדֵי.
מֵיבִּי תּוּמָרוֹ יוּ מֵי גוֹ.״

LESSON 8

Exercise 3, page 63

N: נ; ן; נ; ן
CH: ח; ךְ; כ; ח
M: מ; ם; מ; ם; מ
TS: צ; ץ; צ; ץ
F: פ; ף; פ; ף
Silent: א; ע; ע; א

Exercise 4, page 63

1. נָפַל עַיִן נָתַתָּ אֵין בֵּין
2. מָגֵן אֵם מֶלֶךְ מוֹצֶה עָרִים
3. מֶלֶךְ בָּכָה הֹלֵךְ דֶּרֶךְ שׁוֹכֵן
4. צֶדֶק אֶרֶץ צִיּוֹן מָצָה עֵץ
5. סֵפֶר אָסַף רֹדֵף יָפֶה וּפַר

Exercise 6, page 64

1. מֹדִים מוֹדִם
2. גֹּנֵב גּוֹנֵיו
3. יַחַד יָכָד
4. אֶרֶו עֶרֶב
5. דֹּרוֹט דּוֹרוֹת
6. סֵפֶר שֵׁיפֶר
7. עֵצִים אֵיצִם
8. כֹּל קוֹל

LESSON 9

Exercise 2, page 73 (Some of these words may be spelled in other ways.)

1. בְּנִפּוֹל
2. מְרִין מְרִן
3. סְדֵית שְׁדֵית
4. פְּרֵיד פְּרֵד
5. קְלוֹן כְּלֹן
6. טֶזְדֵי

Exercise 3, page 74

1. נָסְעוּ נָשְׂאוּ
2. עַפְכַּד אַפְקִיד
3. תַּכְלִית טָחְלִת
4. בְּבֵית בְּוֵט
5. סְלַח שְׁלָךְ
6. יִרְעַא יִרְאָה
7. מִצְוָה מִצְבַע
8. אֲבוֹת עֲבוֹט
9. שָׁבַח שָׁנַךְ
10. רָאָה רָעָה
11. אֶפָּקֵד אֶפָּקֵד
12. בְּנֶךְ בְּנֶךְ

Exercise 4, page 75

1. גְּדוֹלָה בְּרִית זְמַן נְשָׁמָה צְדָקָה
2. שׁוֹמְרִים זֹכְרִים הֹלְכִים מַלְכוּת
3. כָּתְבוּ נָסְעוּ יָשְׁבוּ שָׁפְטוּ גָּנְבוּ
4. אֶפְקֹד אֶלְמַד תִּרְכַּב יִזְכֹּר נִדְבַּק
5. כְּתֹב מְלֹךְ שְׁמַע שְׁלַח פְּתַח קְצֹר
6. מִשְׁכָּב לִפְנֵי מִדְבַּר מִשְׁכָּן מִנְחָה

Exercise 5, page 75

1. hear!
2. Israel
3. doorpost
4. menorah
5. blessing
6. righteousness
7. Jerusalem
8. to life
9. Abraham
10. Isaac
11. Jacob
12. commandment
13. happiness
14. prayer
15. Hanukkah

LESSON 10

Exercise 4, page 85

1. הָ/עֲ/בוֹ/דָה וַ/עֲ/טֶ/רֶת
הַ/שָּׁ/מַ/יִם אֱ/לֹ/הִים
2. בַּ/עֲ/גָ/לָא נֶ/חֱ/מָ/טָא
הוֹ/שִׁי/עֵ/נוּ
3. יַמְ/לִיךְ יִתְ/גַּ/דַּל שֶׁ/יִשְׁ/מַע
מַשְׁ/בִּי/עַ
4. תַּלְ/מִי/דִים אַבְ/רָ/הָם בִּשְׁ/מֵי
אֶשְׁ/מַע